Starting from

"No"

D0870373

Starting from

"No"

10 Strategies
to Overcome Your *Fear of Rejection*
and Succeed in Business

AZRIELA JAFFE

DEARBORN™
A **Kaplan Professional** Company

This publication is designed to provide accurate and authoritative information in regard to the subject matter covered. It is sold with the understanding that the publisher is not engaged in rendering legal, accounting, or other professional service. If legal advice or other expert assistance is required, the services of a competent professional person should be sought.

Acquisitions Editor: Jean Iversen
Managing Editor: Jack Kiburz
Interior Design: Lucy Jenkins
Cover Design: Design Alliance, Inc.
Typesetting: the dotted i

Published by Dearborn, a Kaplan Professional Company

Printed in the United States of America

99 00 01 10 9 8 7 6 5 4 3 2 1

Library of Congress Cataloging-in-Publication Data
Jaffe, Azriela.
    Starting from "No" : 10 strategies to overcome your fear of rejection and succeed in business / Azriela Jaffe
        p.   cm.
    Includes bibliographical references and index.
    ISBN 1-57410-122-6
    1. New business enterprises—Management.   2. Success in business.   3. Small business—Management.   I. Title.
    HD62.5.J34   1999
    658.02′2—dc21   99-12698
                                                            CIP

Dearborn books are available at special quantity discounts to use as premiums and sales promotions, or for use in corporate training programs. For more information, please call the Special Sales Manager at 800-621-9621, ext. 4514, or write to Dearborn Financial Publishing, Inc., 155 North Wacker Drive, Chicago, IL 60606-1719.

Dedication

This book is dedicated to my three children, Sarah, Elana, and Elijah, who light up my life and my soul and give me my greatest purpose for being. I love you!

Contents

Acknowledgments

I have much love and appreciation for my husband, Stephen, who first inspired the idea for this book and has always supported my writing dreams. He's the best partner a lady could ask for.

Dave Carpenter, cartoonist extraordinaire, lent many hours to this project and took an otherwise very serious subject and lightened it up for us all. Thanks, Dave!

Pam Lontos, sales trainer extraordinaire, wrote the foreword for this book and gave me her enthusiasm from the start. I much appreciated having the full blessing of a sales expert like Pam. Thanks, Pam!

Thanks to the enthusiastic and knowledgeable staff at Dearborn for catching the vision for this book and guiding it through to publication.

Thanks to Leslie Levine for leading me to my publisher.

I have great appreciation for Scott Smith, president of EntrepreneurPR ("America's #1 Small Business PR Firm"), for leading me to so many outstanding interview sources.

Many thanks to Kathy Wasong, my neighbor, friend, and computer guru, who rescued me from far too many computer disasters.

Gratitude to Anne Wilkinson, student intern, who spent many hours helping me in the research stage of this book, typing countless pages of notes into my computer. Thanks, Anne!

My appreciation goes to the following people, who read my manuscript in draft form and gave me their insightful feedback to help shape the final product you now read: Stephen Jaffe, Ken Knouse, Deb Haggerty, Leslie Levine, Lee Simonson, and Hilton Johnson. (A special acknowledgment to Ken Knouse, who read every word of this book as if it were his own and gave me fabulous feedback from a salesperson in the trenches.)

This book is based on my research, including interviews and e-mail exchanges with the entrepreneurs listed below, who shared candidly about their business experiences and feelings about rejection. Their input is related throughout the book, with credit, or disguised and composited, depending on the circumstances. Thanks to all of the following people who made this book what it is:

Alex Grabenstein, Vintage Lumber Company
Alex Von Allmen and Tania Von Allmen, LogoLab
Bob Leduc, sales consultant
Carol Susan Roth, literary agent and publishing consultant
Chan Martinez, Bondurant School of High Performance
    Driving
Chris McIntyre, EagleRider Motorcycle Rental
Christie Jarvis, independent marketing representative,
    Watkins
Dave Markham, Venture Outdoors
David Oakes, trainer, Fred Pryor Seminars
David Goldsmith, president, Customer Edge
Doug Erickson, Capitol Modular, Inc.
Erik Deckers, humor columnist
Eric Lineback, Johnny Appleseed
Eva Rosenberg, tax professional
Forrest Billington, San Bernardino County Sheriffs
    Department

Greg Jenkins and Tom Neighbors, Bravo Productions
Gretchen Plemmons, Cyber-Pet
Grover Gouker, public speaker
Hilton Johnson, sales coach
Ida Bialik, Women in Business, Inc.
Jacques Worth, High Probability Selling
James Zoppe, American Jousting Alliance
Joanna Slan, author and professional speaker
John Knowlton, founder and editor, *Business@Home*
    magazine
John Scherer, consultant and author
Judy Feld, business and professional coach
Karen Harris, Carolina Publishing Company
Katherine Garbera, romance author
Kathie Hightower, author and professional speaker
Kathy Whittington, area manager, Arbonne International
Kay Rice, Brush Ranch Camp
Kenneth Keller, marketing guru, Keller and Associates
Laura Douglas, marketing analyst
Leslie Levine, author and public relations specialist
Linda Donelson, author and publisher
Maggie Ferrari, Ferrari Color, Inc.
Marcia Tysseling, Star Wares on Main
Marsha Oritt, Investigations Worldwide
Mark Good, Sandler Business Institute
Mark Nelson, independent distributor, FORMOR
    International
Nancy Roebke, ProfNet, Inc.
Pamela Demarest, Launder Dog
Patti Danos, public relations specialist
Pete Masterson, Aeonix Publishing Group
Raman Chauhan, Himalayan Hemp
Rebecca Zenk, Becca's Color Your Own Ceramics
Rick MacDonald, M&M Tee Times

Rick Gardner, Private Party Cars
Robert Gottesman, chiropractor
Robert Prevost, Interactive Motorsports Entertainment
    Corporation
Russell Wild, freelance writer and author
Stacy Brice, president and founder, "Assist U"
Steve Richards, Dealer Advantage Group
Susan Pilgrim, Ph.D., professional speaker and author
Sharon Tucci, independent marketing director, Watkins
Terri Bowersock, Consign and Design Furnishings
Terry Baker, Chugwater Chili, Inc.
Tom Wischmeyer, The Golf University
Turnando Fuad, NSNET/David Goldsmith, president,
    Customer Edge

Foreword

By Pam Lontos

You are so excited! Your career or business looks like a dream come true. That dream, however, can be shattered as you receive more and more rejection.

Everybody in every business has suffered rejection. Most people take the rejection of their services or products as rejection of themselves, as people. In all but the most hardy, this attitude kills their excitement and eventually dampens their profits.

This doesn't need to happen. Rejection is never as pleasant as acceptance, but it can be handled constructively. It's not the rejection but how you react to it that's the problem. If you see rejection as a part of success rather than the end of the world, your reaction will be more positive. Everyone gets rejected. Rejection is the price you pay for success.

This book will help you achieve that success and deal with the noes in life. A no isn't final. It is just part of the process that leads to a yes. People often are afraid to make a decision, so they tell you no, even if they want your product or service. Too many businesspeople simply take the no at face value and quit too early.

Clearly, if you are not equipped to handle rejection, you are not equipped to handle the business environment successfully. This problem is farther reaching than you might first think. Of course, all of the traditional forms of sales comes to mind when you think of rejection: retail, wholesale, inside, outside. But what about the artist trying to get a gallery to show her work? Or the middle manager trying to get the board of directors to adopt one of his ideas? Or an author trying to find a publisher? Everyone who wants something from someone else is in business—the business of getting that someone to fulfill his needs.

Rejection is an integral part of life. Learning how to handle rejection sets the stage for fantastic success and puts you on the path to riches. What dreams have you not pursued because you fear rejection? Is this stopping you from becoming the best you can be? *Starting from "No"* gives you tips on identifying the roots of your fear, changing your mental limitations, adapting to the changes in your life, and much more.

Do you see in yourself some of the effects of the fear of rejection? Well, cheer up! You have in your hands the definitive manual for learning how to get out of the grasp of that fear. By the time you're finished reading and doing the exercises, you will understand the root of your fears and how to overcome them. You will step out into the sunshine of a fulfilling business life—a life where you can pursue your goals without having to step on others to achieve them.

It's not always easy, but you can learn that the more noes you encounter in life, the more yeses you get, too. The possibility of rejection always looms when you take risks, but taking risks also allows greater exposure to the joys of hearing yes. Imagine where you can go and what you can accomplish when you abolish the fear of rejection from your life. Read on and begin a better business life now.

ntroduction

Stephen J. was elated when he walked out of his office cubicle for what he expected would be the last time. With his wife's encouragement, he had quit his full-time job as an accountant to launch a consulting practice, finally pursuing a long-held dream of making it on his own. Stephen looked forward to the fivefold increase in his income and the freedom he dreamed lay ahead. He whistled while he organized his new home office, meticulously designing his company stationery and bookkeeping systems on the computer. After a month of preparation, he was ready. It was time to find some clients.

Shephen picked up the phone that first day, eager to begin. Suddenly, the phone weighed 50 pounds; he had to put it back down. He wasn't going to be one of those salespersons who bothered everyone he knew. The idea of selling to his family and friends made him feel a little queasy. His throat felt thick. Suddenly, the garden needed tending. The kitchen sink needed fixing. Maybe he'd make a few calls tomorrow instead. He would investigate joining some business and community organizations and locate new clients through networking. He knew he had a great program to offer that could save his clients thousands of dollars. All he had to do was prospect. Maybe tomorrow.

A few months later, Stephen had performed admirably for some clients, but they were few and far between. It wasn't getting any easier to pick up the telephone. He was an accountant, not a salesperson; he needed help learning how to sell his services. Stephen invested a few thousand dollars in sales training and coaching. He moved out of the home office to a less distracting environment that would be more conducive to prospecting.

Stephen didn't want to let his wife down. He didn't want to disappoint his kids. He didn't want to return to a corporate job. He had serious incentive to make this work.

Three sales coaches and several months later, clients were still scarce, and Stephen's self-esteem and bank account had taken a nose dive. Now armed with an arsenal of sales techniques, all this motivational talk made him feel that he should be able to sell his services to anyone. Yet he still couldn't pick up the phone to prospect for clients. Stephen, a brilliant accountant and an aspiring entrepreneur with a valuable service, had run across an obstacle he didn't predict and couldn't overcome: *fear of rejection.*

Eighteen months after he launched his business, Stephen reluctantly closed the venture and returned to a corporate job as an accountant. In time, because he was well-respected by his clients, he probably would have acquired enough new business through word of mouth and referral that he could have prospered as an entrepreneur. Time, however, had run out. Stephen's wife had a once-in-a-lifetime career opportunity that necessitated her quitting her corporate job—the one that was largely supporting the family. The couple had three children to support, with another on the way. They could no longer wait for Stephen to prevail over his fear of rejection.

I know all too well the suffering of entrepreneurs like Stephen. Stephen is my husband. Our experience as a new entrepreneurial couple spawned my first book, *Honey, I Want to Start My Own Business: A Planning Guide for Couples,* published by HarperBusiness in 1996. Stephen's difficulties planted the seeds for this book, but confronting my own battles with rejection and criticism as an author, a columnist, and a professional speaker most inspired me to write it.

Before I became a full-time author and speaker, I took two stabs at being an entrepreneur; both efforts were thwarted by my inability to handle rejection. In the mid-1980s, I experienced fabulous health benefits from taking a product manufactured by a network marketing company. As occurs for many multilevel marketers, my excitement about the product's results stimulated me to spread the word to my friends and family, thus launching a part-time network marketing business quite naturally. After I sold the product to everyone I knew who would listen to me, it was time for me to sell to strangers. That's when my fledgling business dried up. I wound up consuming several cases of the product over the next few years.

The following year, the entrepreneurial bug bit me again. I moved from a full-time position as a human resources director for a major corporation to that of a human resources consultant. I lined up my first consulting assignment before I quit my job to make the transition easier on my bank account. Six months later, however, I accepted a position as the company's new full-time human resources director. The temptation to stay in a comfortable corporate job was too great.

It was only when I acquired a motivation strong enough to overcome my rejection phobia—the drive to publish my first book—that I was able to quit my corporate job and become a successful entrepreneur. As a published author and speaker, I encounter plenty of rejection and criticism, but my motivation to succeed is now strong enough to propel me to do the personal growth work necessary to become rejection-proof.

Confronting my fears of rejection and criticism was the most significant challenge to my success as a self-employed professional. My career as an author, a columnist, and a speaker would have been flattened in a short time if I hadn't learned how to manage this emotional roller coaster. I didn't have the luxury of years of therapy or months of coaching. I had to pull it off when my career demanded it—when *Honey, I Want to Start My Own Business* was launched on the national scene and my work was being publicly reviewed, and when I was a frequent guest on radio and television and speaking to audiences around the country. My performance is evaluated constantly.

I still confront my dread of rejection and criticism every day. Though I project an air of self-confidence and command of my subject, behind the professional facade is a sensitive woman who cares deeply about pleasing her audience and meeting the expectations and needs of her clients and readers. I don't want to rid myself of that sensitivity; it's what makes my work unique and well-received in the entrepreneurial community. Instead, I have learned to harness the best of my responsive nature without letting this potential weakness demolish my entrepreneurial dreams.

Two pivotal moments in my career taught me a valuable lesson and solidified my commitment to writing *Starting from No.*

In 1997, bleary-eyed at 6:00 AM, I logged on to my Internet provider to respond to a few e-mail messages. I opened one from a particularly devoted newsletter subscriber, and I was disturbed to read: "I just read your most recent newsletter. It isn't up to your standards. I know that you are busy, but you really should be careful about rushing too much when you put the newsletter out."

My reflexive response was to feel hurt, shame, and fear. The mental noise began immediately: "What if everyone on the newsletter list feels the same way? Maybe this issue isn't any good at all. Gee, I remember offering lots of helpful tips—what is she talking about?" Had I fallen short in a larger way, or did I simply fail to meet this subscriber's preferences and needs in this particular issue?

I discovered later that a glitch in cyberspace resulted in only half of this newsletter being delivered to subscribers. Other subscribers kindly said: "We love your newsletter so much, we don't want to miss any of it. Please send the complete issue." The other woman assumed I had done a poor job and quickly criticized me, without giving me the benefit of the doubt. I took her criticism to heart until I realized the source of the problem was in the newsletter's delivery, not in my performance. Like many people, my first assumption had been to worry that it was my fault.

A few weeks later, I facilitated a weekend workshop for couples involved in a network marketing company. It was magic—lots of fun, learning, insight, and healing. The stack of evaluation forms consisted of nines and tens, and I felt great about the seminar results. What stuck with me for days, though, was one participant's comment on one evaluation form. She noted this short sentence: "You need a new wardrobe." The rest of her evaluation was extremely positive, but apparently she didn't like my appearance. Maybe she didn't like the color blue, or perhaps she thought I was too thin, or too fat, or too pretty, or too ugly, or who knows what. For months following that statement, when I dressed for a public appearance, I critiqued myself in the mirror through her eyes—and I don't even know who she is or what her specific criticism was.

Despair washed over me for some time as I imagined thousands of clients, subscribers, readers, and audience members holding up their personal standards for me to maintain, looking at me with expectation and judgment as they cast their votes for what I should and shouldn't write, speak, wear, even think. How would I ever satisfy so many individual preferences? Would I ever be good enough? My subscriber had said the newsletter wasn't up to my standards, but it was. The seminar participant had said she didn't like the way I was dressed. On that particular day, however, I was wearing one of my favorite dresses, and I felt beautiful. As an entrepreneur, I set my own standards, and I realized I was satisfied with my performance in both of these instances.

When you run a business or appear in the public eye, someone, somewhere always has something critical to say about your work. You can't escape criticism, no matter how perfect you try to be. I finally learned to listen and evaluate criticism, take the best and learn from it, and leave the rest and move on. I can't please everyone with everything I do, and that is OK. It was when I really "got that" that I was propelled to write this book, to help others who still quake from their fear of rejection and criticism.

Perhaps you picked up this book because a paralyzing terror of rejection keeps you from selling, prospering, and contributing your best to the world. Maybe prospecting strangers doesn't phase you, but you unravel when a customer or an employee complains. Even if you are wildly successful in your business, you might wish the sales and customer service process could be less stressful for you.

When confronted with a deeply rooted fear or a formidable obstacle, most people abandon their dreams. I commend you for having the courage to face your greatest fears. The good news is that the fear of rejection is largely learned. What is learned can be unlearned. By reading *Starting from "No"* you will acquire new techniques for calming your mind and facing your fears without having a melt-down. You will learn from other businessmen and businesswomen how to create a business that *minimizes* the likelihood of rejection and complaints, even if you can't eliminate them altogether. You will better understand the source of your sensitivity and what to do about it. Rejection will cease being a monster that can destroy you and will take its proper place among all of your other daily challenges, like managing cash flow, employee turnover, and product development. When rejection loses its emotional charge, you can function at your best.

So let's go slay this dragon called "Rejection"—or better yet, let's just come to peace with it instead.

Identify the Roots
of Your Fear

FEAR OF REJECTION IS A MISNOMER

As a self-employed professional or salesperson, you confront your fears of rejection every single day. Fear of rejection probably has pervaded your life experience so frequently you can't even imagine what your life would be like if the emotional charge were gone and you didn't care about being rejected.

Let me begin this book with a controversial statement: *There is no such thing as fear of rejection.* You've attached yourself to an expression that is heard so frequently in our society that you've come to believe the concept actually exists. Think about it—you aren't really afraid of rejection because rejection, by itself, can't hurt you. What you really fear is what you believe will happen if you are rejected.

This is not a question of semantics but an essential shift in perception. Imagine you went to the doctor and complained, "Doctor, I don't feel well." In response, the doctor didn't ask you about the symptoms but rather simply replied, "I'm going to write you a prescription. Take four pills twice a day for ten days, and you should feel better." You might feel reassured that the doctor was going to solve your problem for you, and in fact the placebo effect might make you feel better. But what if the doctor gave you headache medicine for a stomachache? What if she prescribed twice or half the dose you need to treat the symptoms? What if the medicine only exacerbated your condition or didn't get rid of the underlying problem creating the illness? You could end up in worse shape than before you sought your doctor's help. An effective doctor would ask you enough questions to understand the source of your illness and how it was manifesting itself before she prescribed treatment.

If you march forward looking for the cure to your fear of rejection without understanding what you *actually* are afraid of, you likely will spend a whole lot of money on cures that sound great but don't work for you. No matter how good a particular headache medication may be, if the problem resides in your stomach, it won't do a darn thing for you. Likewise, if your fear of rejection is really a fear of going broke and ending up homeless, your remedy will look a lot different than if your fear of rejection originates from the dread of losing your father's approval if your business fails.

This chapter will help you identify the roots of your fear of rejection and offer some tips for addressing the primary concern that is "running" you. Once you know what ails you and how it affects your business success, you can choose the best remedy for treating the problem or the most effective vaccination for preventing the distress in the first place.

Compiled in the next several pages is a brief summary of six different fears that often underlie the fear of rejection. Read each description and the illustration that accompanies it. Take each self-test and identify which fear or fears are your strongest inhibitors.

1. FEAR OF FAILURE— THE PERFECTIONISTIC PROFESSIONAL

You can trace the roots of your perfectionism all the way back to grade school, when less than an "A" on your report card was unacceptable to either you or your parents. You would cry in frustration when you couldn't master a skill quickly, and you rarely took on an endeavor unless you were sure you would excel. As an adult, you have adopted your own high standards of behavior for yourself and those who work and live with you. Family, business partners, and employees may accuse you of holding unreasonably high expectations.

By trying to be perfect in everything you do, you erroneously believe that you will avoid rejection. You hope that by performing your work perfectly or by delivering the ideal sales presentation, you will never hear the words, "I'm not interested in what you have to offer." Which really means to you, "You aren't good enough for me." Which implies, "You aren't good." If perfectionism runs you, you allow potential

? SELF-TEST: *FEAR OF FAILURE*
■ ■ ■

Answer yes or no to each question.

1. I frequently rehash in my mind how I should have or could have done something better. ____ yes ____ no

2. In school, I always got top grades. ____ yes ____ no

3. When I make a mistake, I fret about it for a long time. ____ yes ____ no

4. When an employee or a family member makes a mistake, I can be too hard on him. ____ yes ____ no

5. I can't stand when work is sloppy, late, disorganized, or not up to expectations. ____ yes ____ no

6. When I was a young child, my parents were distressed if I didn't get "As" or do my chores perfectly. ____ yes ____ no

7. My number one priority as a child was to meet my parents' expectations and to be sure I never disappointed them. ____ yes ____ no

8. I tend to set realistic goals that I am fairly sure I can achieve. ____ yes ____ no

9. I believe that the best way to avoid rejection is to always do my best. ____ yes ____ no

10. It is hard for me to delegate to anyone because I usually think I can do it better myself. ____ yes ____ no

Score: _____ (Tally the number of yeses.)

■■**?**

customers to be judge and jury of your worthiness—the same power you gave your parents long ago. No wonder you fear rejection.

- **Your fear of rejection masks:** Fear of failure.
- **Your motto is:** "Do it right, or don't do it at all."
- **Your positive intention is:** Avoid rejection by delivering excellent work.
- **The ineffective result is:** Paralysis by analysis. You likely miss out on opportunities because if you aren't absolutely sure you will excel, you hesitate to develop a new skill, prospect a new client, or bring out an innovative product. In this competitive age, narrowing your business to only what you can guarantee will be successful is dangerous. You will stop developing new talent and expertise and risk becoming obsolete.

Harry, an architect, exemplifies this profile:

My perfectionism drives my wife and employees nuts. If the checking account doesn't balance to the penny, I'll work on it for hours just to balance it, and I've been known to yell at my wife for not making the proper entry into the checking account. If employees mess something up, I tend to come down too hard on them. I know they are only human—mistakes happen—and I should be more forgiving. But they usually have done something stupid that I never would have done if I were doing the job myself. I can't stand stupid people. When a prospective client turns me down, I usually think that if I had done a better sales job, the prospect would have bought. When a customer complains, I assume that there was something we could have done to prevent that customer from being unhappy. I'm always trying to improve myself and my business, which keeps me motivated, but makes it difficult for me to relax.

Keep in mind. No matter how much you use perfectionism to avoid rejection, you still will be criticized, and your services will be declined time and again, as long as you conduct business. Let's say for argument's sake that you *are* perfect in delivering your service or making your sales presentation. You still will hear the words "not interested." Why? Customer preferences. Your product may be priced too high, the wrong color, not available fast enough, not targeted to the consumer's exact needs, and so on. No matter how perfect you are, your service or product will be the right match for only a narrow segment of the population, and you always will have an imperfect knowledge of your customers and prospects, no matter how much effort you make to get to know them. *Perfectionism as a mechanism for avoiding rejection never works.* You will never, *ever* be good enough to please the entire world!

 **TRY THIS!**

Delegate a task that you normally hold onto, and keep your objections to yourself if it's not done perfectly. (The task can be work-related or household-related.) Start with something that doesn't hold a lot of significance for you, and see whether you can lessen your emotional need to have the task performed perfectly and according to your standards. The next time you or someone in your business makes a mistake, lighten up. Remind yourself that it's only work, money, one job, one prospect saying no, whatever. Keep your disappointment in perspective.

 **TRY THIS!**

To free yourself from the constraints of taking on only projects in which you will excel, pursue a hobby or an endeavor that you know you might enjoy, even if you won't shine at it. For example, I enrolled in a watercolor painting class once, although my artistic abilities leave much to be desired. Even though no one was going to see my finished product but me, and no income was riding on it, it was still hard for me to relax and enjoy the experience of painting without worrying about doing it right. This conditioning is difficult to break; be patient with yourself and keep working at it.

- **Your new motto could be:** "Lighten up. It's only a mistake."

2. FEAR OF SUCCESS— THE SABOTAGING PROFESSIONAL

Have you considered the possibility that what appears to be your fear of rejection is really a clever disguise for the fear of success? Preposterous, you think. Why would any business professional be afraid to succeed? It's not success per se, but what prosperity, abundant work, and recognition bring with them that you may not be ready for. Maybe you'd have to work harder than you do now, and you like your leisure time. Perhaps you realize that once you are committed to something or someone, you will be held accountable for delivering. You might suffer from the imposter syndrome— the fear that people expect more of you than you can give and you'll be exposed as an imposter when you can't measure

? SELF-TEST: *FEAR OF SUCCESS*
■■■

Answer yes or no to each question.

1. As soon as I achieve a certain amount of success, something bad seems to happen. ____ yes ____ no

2. People often describe me as an underachiever with great potential. ____ yes ____ no

3. I know I'm capable of achieving more, but something blocks me. ____ yes ____ no

4. I present myself as self-assured and knowledgeable, but deep down I'm afraid I'll be exposed as incompetent. ____ yes ____ no

5. I have trouble figuring out what I'm really worth and a fair price to charge for my services or product. ____ yes ____ no

6. I tend to run away from commitments, especially long-term ones. ____ yes ____ no

7. As a child, my self-esteem was very low. ____ yes ____ no

8. I don't really want to work too hard. ____ yes ____ no

9. I worry that if I make a lot of money and become really successful, I might not be a kind, spiritual person who is available for my spouse and children. ____ yes ____ no

10. Someone important in my life is threatened by my success or doesn't believe in me, so I sabotage myself to retain that relationship. ____ yes ____ no

Score: _____ (Tally the number of yeses.)

...?

up. Your desire for success may conflict with core beliefs that you are unworthy, and you may sabotage your efforts to keep your business results aligned with what you believe about yourself. Fear of rejection may be an unconscious weapon for thwarting your ambivalent attempt to succeed.

If you suffer from a fear of success, you feed yourself many rational lies (rationalizations) and excuses for why you aren't doing what it takes to be successful, including: "I'm afraid of rejection!" Ask yourself this question: Do you lack the skills and capital required to achieve your business goals, or are you *unwilling* to do what it takes? The end result is the same, but you should not confuse unwillingness with inability. If unwillingness is your steady companion, you may be subtly or unconsciously sabotaging yourself.

- **Your fear of rejection masks:** The fear of what you might lose or have to undergo if you become successful.
- **Your motto is:** "I'm almost where I want to be."
- **Your positive intention is:** To keep your business performance aligned with your deepest beliefs and fears so you don't have to abandon your comfort zone.
- **The ineffective result is:** If you keep setting higher goals and never reaching them, or if you continue to wreck excellent progress when you close in on success, you'll always feel frustrated, as will the people who live and work with you.

Maggy, a life insurance salesperson, exemplifies this profile:

I hear my colleagues complaining about how much they hate cold calling. Funny, for me, cold calling is easy. Most people don't want my services; they usually are strangers, and expectations of me are low. I'm much more nervous when I get a strong lead to someone who knows me (or knows someone who knows me) or when I'm putting together a big deal with a guy who is my father's age. Suddenly, I feel like a little kid and I wonder whether the client is going to figure out that I don't know what the heck I'm talking about. I know I'm supposed to "fake it till I make it," especially when I'm negotiating with a high-wealth individual, but I keep thinking he's going to see right through my business suit to this little girl in pigtails and a jumper, crying for her blankie. The last few times I was close to landing lucrative deals, I messed it up by not following through in a timely way or not asking the right questions, and I lost the clients. It's hard for me to believe in my own success, so when a client I place on a pedestal puts his faith in me, I feel very uncomfortable.

Keep in mind. If you suffer from an unconscious need to sabotage your success, the money you pour into sales training and coaching to address your fears of rejection either may be wasted dollars or may backfire on you when the techniques start working! The better you get at sales, the more you fight against yourself. If you really are hooked in this syndrome, seek professional help, not from a sales coach but from a good therapist, to help you break out of the vicious cycle.

 **TRY THIS!**

Pay attention to what circumstances trigger your inner saboteur. The saboteur may show up as a nasty or sarcastic voice in your head, an unhealthy pattern like procrastination, or some life event that distracts you from fulfilling your business mission. Do certain people or places bring out your insecurities? Can you iden-

" JUST LEAVE HIM ALONE. WE ALL HAVE TO HANDLE
REJECTION IN OUR OWN WAY. "

tify any internal conflict between what you say you want and what you believe you deserve? Keep a journal of your thoughts for several weeks, and you may be able to identify the pattern. ...!

 **TRY THIS!**

The next time you feed yourself a good excuse for not pursuing a business deal, prospecting a new client, or undertaking some other activity to expand your business, rather than writing it off as your fear of rejection, ask yourself whether you receive any payoff when you don't succeed. Are the rewards for *not* reaching your goals more valuable to you than the benefits you receive when you don't achieve what you want? What do you gain as a result of your failure to pursue your business goals?   **...!**

- **Your new motto could be:** "I am ready for all the success I am capable of achieving."

3. FEAR OF BEING HUMILIATED—
THE SELF-CONSCIOUS PROFESSIONAL

Being rejected in business stirs up a great deal of emotional charge for you. It's more than just losing a sale, it's losing your pride as well. Perhaps as a young child, you suffered the merciless taunting of classmates who were intent on humiliating you to tears. For you, rejection was so painful and disgraceful that you carried this emotional baggage into adulthood. Now you anticipate rejection and become self-absorbed as you imagine all the things that a business professional may be thinking or saying about you.

One man I spoke to purchased an accounting franchise for $12,000 against the advice of his father and father-in-law, who questioned the service the franchise would offer. Whenever a prospect said no to this owner, he questioned his judgment in purchasing the franchise and worried about looking like a fool to his father and father-in-law. Every time someone didn't want to buy his services, he berated himself: "Maybe the prospect was right and this service isn't any good. Maybe I *was* an idiot for spending that much money on it." The fear of having made the wrong decision with his financial investment—and maybe even more importantly, looking foolish in front of his family—paralyzed the owner in the selling process.

? ■ ■ ■ SELF-TEST: *FEAR OF BEING HUMILIATED*

Answer yes or no to each question.

1. Criticism is very painful for me because I take it so personally. _____ yes _____ no

2. When I was a small child, classmates teased me, and I often felt humiliated. _____ yes _____ no

3. I will do almost anything to avoid looking like a fool. _____ yes _____ no

4. Others would describe me as a highly sensitive person, and I would agree. _____ yes _____ no

5. I am self-conscious about my appearance. _____ yes _____ no

6. Selling or delivering my service or product in front of a large group is much harder for me than giving a one-on-one presentation. _____ yes _____ no

7. My number one priority as a child was to avoid being rejected and teased by my peers. _____ yes _____ no

8. I tend to stay away from business activities that could leave me feeling embarrassed or ashamed if I'm not well-received. _____ yes _____ no

9. If I made a cold call and the prospect hung up the phone on me, called me names, or slammed the door in my face, I would feel disgraced. _____ yes _____ no

10. If someone criticizes me in front of someone else, I feel greatly embarrassed or ashamed. _____ yes _____ no

Score: _____ (Tally the number of yeses.)

...?

- **Your fear of rejection masks:** The fear of being humiliated.
- **Your motto is:** "I don't want to look like a fool."
- **Your positive intention is:** To avoid feeling the humiliation you felt as a child.
- **The ineffective result is:** You will find prospecting so terrifying, you will be unlikely to make enough sales presentations to prosper in your business. When you do get in front of a prospective client or current customer, you may be so worried about what the prospect or customer thinks about you, you'll have a hard time really listening and learning how your company can best meet the person's needs.

Sheila, an overweight sales rep, exemplifies this profile:

I'm a big woman, and I'm very self-conscious about my appearance. When I was a sales rep many years ago, every time I had to call on a new or prospective customer, I was terrified of what he would be thinking or saying about me as soon as I left. I'd find excuses not to make the call, or I'd stall between appointments. After being consumed by this fear for five years, I got some professional help and my therapist helped me understand. What was I afraid of? Someone was going to tell me that I'm fat? Big deal; I know that! What's the worst possible thing that could happen? Once I gave a presentation to 400 other sales reps. I was terrified that I would get up to the podium and not be able to say a word. That's exactly what happened—I froze! I experienced my worst fear, and guess what—I survived. Embarrassment won't kill you.

Keep in mind. Because you equate rejection with humiliation, of course you aim to minimize the amount of rejection you receive. However, your ability to tune into a prospect's needs is diminished when you are unduly worried about how you look, sound, and perform. This self-absorption lessens your effectiveness as a salesperson and, ironically, leads you to more of the rejection that you try to avoid. When I entered the speaking circuit as a professional speaker, one of the best pieces of advice I heard was this: When you look out at that huge sea of faces and you are scared to death about your performance, shift your focus from trying to *impress* the audience to how you can best *serve* them. When you take the focus off of yourself and place it where it belongs—on the client—you will be much more effective.

TRY THIS!

Enroll in an acting, a dance, or another class that forces you to confront your phobia of looking like a fool. Imagine taking a belly-dancing class at the local adult education center. Or how about trying your hand at improvisational comedy? If you suffer from a fear of rejection and humiliation, you might rather die than do such a thing. Consider confronting this fear in an arena where you have little to lose, no income at stake, and no important client to impress. As you begin to understand that you can survive looking silly, or you do not always have to do everything perfectly in front of an audience, you can bring this new found courage to the business arena.

TRY THIS!

When you are plagued with thoughts of how awful it would be if you were humiliated, write down exactly what you fear. Get as specific as possible. For example: "I'm afraid that when I go to the chamber of commerce networking event, I will sit at a table by myself and no one will talk to me." Then what? "I'm afraid that people will think I must be weird because no one wants to sit next to me." And then what? "I'm afraid that. . . ." Get the idea? If you use this writing exercise to take your fears to the end, you probably will discover that even your worst fear is no big deal, something you can handle, or not likely to occur.   ■■■!

- ■ **Your new motto could be:** "What's the worst that can happen? Whatever it is, I'll accept it and make the best of it."

4. FEAR OF NOT BEING LIKED OR NOT RECEIVING APPROVAL—THE PEOPLE-PLEASING PROFESSIONAL

You may be drawn to sales and your profession precisely *because* you love interacting with customers and clients. Your gregarious nature, friendly demeanor, and easy-going manner might make others surprised to hear that you harbor a fear of rejection. Your primary desire in life, perhaps even more than earning a prosperous living, is to be liked and included in a social circle of friends, neighbors, and family. When your business supports that need, you feel great. When selling or prospecting threatens your craving to be accepted, admired, appreciated, and respected, you feel shaky.

We've all heard the expression "Don't take it personally" when it comes to handling rejection. You take every no or complaint to heart because it threatens your self-image as a person everybody likes. Your worst nightmare is to be viewed as arrogant or to unintentionally offend someone. You can trace this pattern back to childhood.

? ∎∎∎ **SELF-TEST:** *FEAR OF NOT BEING LIKED OR NOT RECEIVING APPROVAL*

Answer yes or no to each question.

1. Having a number of close friends and colleagues who respect me is important to me. _____ yes _____ no

2. It distresses me when someone I care about, or even a stranger, doesn't approve of me. _____ yes _____ no

3. I know it's unreasonable for me to sell my business to everyone, but I have a hard time accepting when someone doesn't want my services or product. _____ yes _____ no

4. Being popular was important to me as a child. _____ yes _____ no

5. I find it awkward to sell to friends and family. _____ yes _____ no

6. I worry about saying the right thing or interrupting someone when I make a sales pitch. I don't want to offend anyone. _____ yes _____ no

7. I'm concerned that my self-confidence might be mistaken for arrogance. _____ yes _____ no

8. As a child, I was so eager to gain the approval of my parents and my peers that I wouldn't be outspoken about anything controversial. _____ yes _____ no

9. It is very important to me that my current customers and clients like doing business with me and have high regard for me. _____ yes _____ no

10. I may appear outgoing to my colleagues and customers, but I'm more sensitive and shy than they realize. _____ yes _____ no

Score: _____ (Tally the number of yeses.) **∎∎?**

Depending on your profession, you may have an added reason to want everyone to like you. In a profession like mine, one public statement of disapproval of my written work could be devastating. I wait with baited breath for reviews of my books to appear in national publications that carry great merit with bookstores and entrepreneurs. One poor review could decrease sales dramatically, so I can't help but try to please everyone and take any public rejection of my work very seriously.

- **Your fear of rejection masks:** The desire to be highly regarded by everyone.
- **Your motto is:** "How can I please you?"
- **Your positive intention is:** To create a social network that feeds and nurtures your soul.
- **The ineffective result is:** You waste precious energy trying to satisfy people who will never be rewarding friends or customers, no matter how hard you try.

Marge, a professional speaker, exemplifies this profile:

Public speaking is a necessary part of my career as an author and a consultant, so I put myself on the speaking circuit, but it's my least favorite activity. I've been told that I'm quite good at it, and I do have a message that I am passionate about sharing. But it kills me to be standing in front of an entire group of people who are all evaluating me. I want all of them—all 200, or 400, or 1,000 of them—to like me. And not only that, I want them to like everything about me. I want every person in the audience to think I'm beautiful, and articulate, and smart, and you name it. It's torture for me to read the evaluation forms because even if I get all "9s" and "10s", I'm wondering what I did wrong to make someone not like me enough to give me a "10."

Keep in mind. Because your biggest fear may be alienating friends and family, you could be extremely reluctant to sell your product or services to your inner circle. Although most sales professionals begin by networking with the people closest to them, you may be more comfortable starting your business by serving and prospecting strangers and, once your business is launched, conversing with your friends and family only when *they* approach *you* (which they undoubtedly will once you become successful!).

 **TRY THIS!**

Create a close circle of friends and colleagues who affirm your value to them regularly. You need only a few to make a real difference. To ensure that you receive the emotional support and respect you yearn for, take the time to give it as well. Send an e-mail when you see a colleague quoted in the newspaper. Write a letter to an author who moved you or to a business professional who provided you with a valuable service. Get in the habit of giving out praise and appreciation, and you surely will receive more of it as well.

 **TRY THIS!**

I have a folder in my filing cabinet labeled "fan mail." In this folder, I place the letters and e-mails I have received from strangers, colleagues, and friends, praising my work and my valued contribution to their lives. That file is a source of reassurance and solace to me when I have experienced a painful criticism or rejection. Create your own version of a fan mail folder for a day when you need to remind yourself that you are highly regarded and respected.

- **Your new motto could be:** "I am loved and appreciated for who I am and what I contribute to the world."

5. FEAR OF FINANCIAL DISASTER—THE DESPERATE PROFESSIONAL

Like a dog who smells your fear and bites you in response, a prospective customer senses when a business owner or sales professional is desperate, and it kills any chance of doing business with the prospect. No one wants to buy from someone who communicates an unhealthy urgency. The implication is: "If you are desperate for my business, something must be wrong with your product or services. I don't want to chance buying from you if others don't want to." If your physical survival, as well as that of your family, depends on making the next sale, your fear of rejection will be monstrous when the sale demands that you "make it or break it." You aren't really afraid of rejection but, rather, the consequences of not succeeding financially with your endeavor.

- **Your fear of rejection masks:** The fears of dependence, letting down a loved one or an investor, financial bankruptcy, and losing precious possessions.
- **Your motto is:** "God forbid I don't make this sale."
- **Your positive intention is:** To motivate yourself through fear to work harder and do better.
- **The ineffective result is:** You chase away the very customers you hope to attract.

Gary, a network marketing professional, exemplifies this profile:

A strange thing happened to me when I quit my full-time job to build my network marketing business. For

? ■■■ SELF-TEST: *FEAR OF FINANCIAL DISASTER*

Answer yes or no to each question.

1. My spouse or children depend on me to be successful.
   ____ yes ____ no

2. I have slim savings and assets to fall back on if I don't pull in the cash I need every month. ____ yes ____ no

3. I have significant household and business overhead expenses to meet every month. ____ yes ____ no

4. If I don't improve my performance or revenue significantly, I fear that I will go out of business or have to get a new job. ____ yes ____ no

5. I think sometimes a prospect can tell how desperate I feel when I pitch my services or product. ____ yes ____ no

6. I wake up in the middle of the night or can't fall asleep because I'm worried about finances. ____ yes ____ no

7. My spouse (or in-laws, parents, or business partner) is upset about our financial situation and is giving me a hard time. ____ yes ____ no

8. I catastrophize and worry about extremes, like losing the house or my spouse, even though that's highly unlikely.
   ____ yes ____ no

9. When I lose one sale or a prospect says no, I generalize and panic about not being able to earn the money I need.
   ____ yes ____ no

10. The more desperate my financial situation, the harder it is to prospect because my self-esteem falls into the gutter.
    ____ yes ____ no

Score: _____ (Tally the number of yeses.) ■■■**?**

two years, I was working my MLM business on the side, moonlighting about ten hours a week. My part-time business was growing faster than I could keep up with, so I took a big leap of faith and quit my day job, thinking I'd replace my salary with my network marketing revenue within six months. Instead, my MLM business started falling off, and I couldn't understand why because I was working harder at it than ever. My upline sponsor helped me see that I was projecting too much fear into every conversation, now that my livelihood depended on the business. I was turning off prospective customers and business builders before they even gave the business a chance. I took on a part-time consulting job in the field where I was formerly employed. That helped relieve the financial pressure so that I could go back to doing what worked so well for me in the first place—telling people why I loved the products so much and piquing their interest in wanting to know more.

Keep in mind. Your fear of rejection is magnified when a spouse and children depend on you or if you have borrowed money to finance your company. You carry the weight of this burden on your shoulders every time you promote yourself and your business. You might consider the possibility of losing an investor's money intolerable, or you may feel great shame in not fulfilling your vow to your mate to contribute your share of household income.

 **TRY THIS!**

A colleague gave me some great advice when I was waiting anxiously for one of my books to sell to a publisher: "Get yourself another stream of income to help take the pressure off." I didn't give up my dream and go back to corporate employment; rather, I secured a consulting contract that provided me with monthly income for a period of time while the painstakingly slow process of a book sale marched forward. I still needed the book to sell, but hoping it would sell within six months, instead of needing it to sell in two months so I could pay the bills, kept me from panicking when the process moved slower than I would have liked.

Look for ways to bring in some monthly revenue, outside of your main business, if you have trouble being profitable with all of your eggs in one basket. A friend of mine, a business consultant who hit a slow period, took a job delivering blood to neighboring hospitals a few evenings a week. Be creative; the solution doesn't even have to lie within your professional field of expertise. If you worry about losing your focus when you get a part-time job or a consulting gig to tide you over, establish some accountabilities and short-term business goals that will keep you on track in your business—even if it doesn't get all of your time. ▪▪▪!

 **TRY THIS!** ▪ ▪ ▪

If you feel pressured by obligations to family or investors, you may be tempted to avoid talking about your difficulties as much as possible. You probably aren't hiding anything from them, so discuss the situation openly, and elicit their support and suggestions. One man I interviewed was too ashamed to tell his wife of his termination from a sales job, so he dressed in his business suit and spent several days at an out-of-town mall so his wife wouldn't know he had been fired. That game lasted only a few weeks, until he ran into his wife's friend at the mall. Ask your spouse or investors for help if you need it. They want you to succeed as much as you do! ▪▪▪!

- **Your new motto could be:** "I have always had enough money to survive in the past, and I will today, too."

6. FEAR OF CHANGE—THE PREDICTABLE PROFESSIONAL

To your peers tucked away in their cubicles and corporate offices, you may appear to be a professional who can handle a certain amount of volatility and unpredictability in your career. Perhaps you have forgone the steady paycheck in exchange for a commission sales position. You may struggle to make your living as a freelance writer, living frugally from assignment to assignment. You may run a seasonal business, with widely fluctuating cash flow. Although unpredictability may be part of the scene for you, within the framework of your profession, you may be rather attached to the status quo. You call on the same clients over and over again. You settle into a daily routine that you've had for years. You live fairly comfortably, though you have not reached your full potential. You don't want to rock the boat.

- **Your fear of rejection masks:** Fear of the unknown.
- **Your motto is:** "Better safe than sorry."
- **Your positive intention is:** To protect the success you have achieved.
- **The ineffective result is:** Your business can, and will, plateau. Over time, as you lose existing clients, if you are reluctant to replace them with new clients (it might change your daily routine or demand something new from you), your business may die a slow death.

? SELF-TEST: *FEAR OF CHANGE*
■■■

Answer yes or no to each question.

1. I go to sleep and get up in the morning at the same time every day. _____ yes _____ no

2. I prefer to eat my meals at about the same time every day. _____ yes _____ no

3. Changes in my daily routine make me uneasy. _____ yes _____ no

4. I believe that change is *not* always for the good. _____ yes _____ no

5. Predictability reassures me. _____ yes _____ no

6. My business (or sales job) has been established for some time. _____ yes _____ no

7. I am reluctant to prospect new clients because I don't know how they will respond. _____ yes _____ no

8. I have been serving a small group of regular clients for some time. _____ yes _____ no

9. I feel anxious if a prospect raises a question or objection I haven't heard before. _____ yes _____ no

10. I would rather be comfortable and earn less money than raise my income and feel unsettled. _____ yes _____ no

Score: _____ (Tally the number of yeses.)

...?

Janet, a freelance writer, exemplifies this profile:

For the past ten years, I have been self-employed as a freelance writer for magazines. My income has been steady, though a few thousand dollars less per year than I really need to be comfortable. I tend to write for the same editors over and over again, and I hesitate to contact any new magazines that might be able to give me work. At first, I thought my fear of rejection was all that was keeping me from sending them queries. But I notice that sometimes I don't even follow up on a warm lead from a colleague. Truth is, my life is pretty predictable these days, and I like that. I know approximately how much work I'll be receiving, how much money I'll be earning, and what my lifestyle will be like. If I started working a lot harder, I don't know if it would be good for my kids. If I earned more money, I don't know if my husband would feel threatened. If I started getting rejected a lot, my self-esteem might plummet. Then I might have trouble writing at all. I don't know what the future would be like if I started trying to get new clients, so I'd rather leave it the way that it is.

Keep in mind. You are unlikely to embrace any new behavior that will disrupt your routine dramatically. You will best surmount what seems like a fear of rejection by becoming more comfortable with change and venturing into the unknown slowly, one step at a time, and by being as prepared as possible. You are the kind of person who wants to minimize surprises and instances of being caught off guard. Be well-rehearsed for your sales calls and extremely knowledgeable about your product. The more you prospect new clients and learn how to respond to a variety of situations, the more comfortable you will feel, as prospecting ceases to be an unknown and unpredictable experience for you.

When you get up the courage to dial the telephone or drop by a prospect's office, don't be surprised if you actually feel relief when the potential client doesn't pick up the phone or isn't available. If you prefer the comfort zone you've created with your existing clients, you are ambivalent about whether you really want a new client to hire you for your services. It is important for you to set business goals that are in concert with your truest desires, or you will set yourself up to fail. Expect that you probably will grow your business slowly, or just enough to keep your bills paid or stay in business.

 TRY THIS!

A scripted sales presentation is a turn-off to a prospective customer when it sounds canned, but you can write out and practice a presentation before approaching a new client to increase your skill level and confidence. If you are a professional speaker, you might write your speech and rehearse it ahead of time, though give the talk more spontaneously and without reading your notes. The key is to reassure yourself that you know what you want to say and that you are well-prepared. Write down common objections you receive, and think through ahead of time how you will respond. Every situation may be unique, but the more you mitigate your fear of the unknown by preparing yourself for every possible outcome, the less afraid of rejection you will be.

 TRY THIS!

Identify the anchors in your daily routine that give you and your family pleasure and stability. Perhaps it's napping in the afternoon, meeting your children when they get off the school bus, or taking a few minutes over coffee to read the paper in the morning. Write down at least ten activities that currently shape your day and make being self-employed worth the struggle. Memorize them, or keep the list handy. You don't want to give any of these up to expand your business. Your fear of rejection will rear its ugly head most when an activity threatens your cherished routines. Look for ways to expand your business without losing any of these anchors, and your fear of rejection may dissipate.   ■■■!

- **Your new motto could be:** "I am well-prepared to handle whatever comes my way."

MOVING FORWARD

If you are like most people, you experience every fear to some degree, but one or two really get in your way.

As we proceed through the rest of the book, keep in mind those profiles where you scored the most yeses. The root cause of your fear of rejection (fear of success or failure, fear of financial loss, fear of not being liked, fear of being humiliated, or fear of change), determines your response to many of the suggestions in this book. Some techniques will resonate strongly—just the medicine the doctor ordered—and some ideas or concepts will feel irrelevant or unnecessary.

Remember how we started this chapter—with the metaphor of you, an ailing patient, seeking your doctor's medical attention. Now that you have a better sense of what generates your fear of rejection, you'll be more likely to seek out and respond to the proper treatment.

CHAPTER 2

Find Your Motivator

ERECTING A FENCE AROUND REJECTION

I don't recommend trying to rid yourself of the fear of rejection. You are kidding yourself if you think that you can take the right sales training course or undergo enough personal therapy that you transform magically into some kind of superman or superwoman who can withstand bullets of rejection without batting an eyelash. I don't believe you even *want* to achieve such a goal. If you ever got that detached, you might also lose the sensitivity and compassion that make you an enjoyable person with whom to do business.

Let go of the notion that you can follow some path or learn some technique in this book that will free you entirely from encountering or battling rejection in your business life. Rather, imagine you grow a large vegetable and flower garden. You spend hours a day in that garden, planting, weeding, mulching, and watering, to nurture the growth of a bountiful harvest. Even if you purchase the best seed and do all the right things to nurture the plants' growth, however, pests like beetles, mice, rabbits, and groundhogs can destroy all of your efforts in a matter of days if you give them the freedom to enter the garden and munch to their hearts' content. What do you, as gardener, do? You buy fences, traps, and repellents, and you do your best to keep these pests from devouring your crop. You accept that these pests exist in the world, but you don't let them destroy your garden.

This metaphor applies to handling rejection in your business. Your motivation is the fence you erect around your business, mind, and soul, so that even when those pests called the "fear of rejection" show up (camouflaged as procrastination, indecision, laziness, confusion, negative thinking, and so on), you can keep them from destroying the business you work so hard to build. Your fence is built of resolution, dedication, commitment, discipline, strength, courage, burning desire, determination, and persistence. Your motivation won't prevent the rejection pests from showing up, but it *will* put them in their proper place—poking their noses through the fence but allowing you to continue to harvest what you sow. The larger and more bountiful your garden, the bigger and more plentiful these pests get, but that's okay. The stronger your business and your self-esteem, the more motivated you will be and the easier it will become to erect a fence high enough to keep the rejection critters from eating away at your profits and peace of mind.

Building your fence starts with making a commitment. When Americans were surveyed about what they wanted to be when they grew up, only 5 percent reported they had any desire to be a salesperson. Although selling is a profession just like accounting, teaching, and law, few people spend the time or money to study how to do it well, or aspire to become the best salespersons they can be. For most people, selling is a necessary evil in business, a job they do until something better comes along, or a last resort because no one would hire them on straight salaries.

I had my first sales position right out of college, working on straight commission for an employment agency. I held a bachelor's degree in social work. It was never my desire to be in sales, but no one would hire me fresh out of college for more than $13,000 a year—not a living wage for a woman living on her own in Boston. I accepted the commission sales job because I hoped that my performance would compensate me with the income I needed to support myself. While in that job, I focused on learning the employment industry, but I recall no effort to better my selling skills or to improve my ability to withstand rejection. I viewed human resources as my profession and selling as what I had to do to earn my paycheck. If I had regarded sales as my profession, I might have stayed in that job longer than the three years I did, or I may have earned an even higher income.

Commit yourself to improving your ability to respond to rejection and criticism with resiliency and fortitude. Determine to be successful in your chosen profession. Pledge to learn how to sell your product or services to the best of your ability. Be willing to commit your time and resources to mastering your field and surmounting any personal obstacles in your way. The rest will follow.

NEGATIVE VERSUS POSITIVE MOTIVATION

Motivation differs from person to person. In this chapter, we'll explore a spectrum of motivations that you may use to keep you on track and focused on your goals. One of the first questions to consider is this: Are you motivated most by moving *toward* what you desire or *away from* what you fear? For some people, fear is a greater motivator than desire. Your anxiety about what you might lose if you don't succeed can propel you to jump over hurdles and suffer some of the pain of rejection. The problem with fear as a motivator is that it can make your life stressful. When fear haunts you every day, it is hard to enjoy your work or to perform effectively. You may be more short-tempered and depressed and less creative.

Other people are motivated most by what they dream of achieving and the rewards they expect to collect when they reach their goals. Although positive visualization and goal setting is essential to business success, the drawback to positive motivations is that they can be vague, elusive, and not powerful enough to get you to do what you need to do *today* to succeed. Fear motivators work better to impel you to do something you don't want to do today. Positive motivators work better to keep you committed for the long term.

You likely will be stimulated by most or all of the following motivators during your career. One trick for handling your fear of rejection and criticism is to shift your focus toward strengthening your motivation for success. What follows naturally is your willingness to do what it takes to succeed, including managing the discomfort of rejection. As you read through the following five motivations, pay attention to those that resonate with you most. Therein lies the clues you need to become more rejection-proof. Try some of the recommended exercises to help you build your motivation fence higher.

1. MOTIVATION: I'LL SHOW YOU

Many successful entrepreneurs have channeled their anger into energy and created phenomenally successful enterprises. Some relish proving to all the parents, teachers, business colleagues, and friends who said that something couldn't be done that indeed it could be, and done well. The authors of the *Chicken Soup for the Soul* series of books were rejected by 35 publishers before Health Communications published their first book. They became multimillionaires, as did the publisher. I bet all of the publishing executives who turned them down are kicking themselves now.

Terri Bowersock, president of Consign and Design Furnishings of Mesa, Arizona, shared with me how the "I'll show you" motivation helped her build a multimillion dollar business:

> I built my business from a $2,000 loan that I got from my grandmother to a $10 million business over an 18-year period of time. The entire business was started because of rejection.

I am severely dyslexic. I graduated from high school spelling at a third-grade level and reading at a fifth-grade level. Throughout grade school and high school, my peers made fun of me. I suffered through two years of college, but it was impossible to manage. I quit, but when I looked for a job, my job applications looked like they were written by a third grader.

I turned rejection into determination. I motivated myself with a persistent dream that I would drive up to my high school class reunion in a limousine. I would be smarter and more successful than any of them. I would show all my old teachers and my peers that my poor grades meant nothing.

Sure enough, I was running a multimillion dollar business when my 20th high school reunion came around. I sponsored some reunion activities and arrived in my Infiniti. I saw a woman I used to put on a pedestal for being the head cheerleader. She's on her fourth divorce. I ran into peers I used to envy for their good grades. Most of them were living everyday lives. As I aspired to for so many years, I had far surpassed everyone in my class.

Golf professional Lisa Ann Horst of Lancaster, Pennsylvania, became infuriated when a sports writer made the sensational and controversial statement that women didn't belong in professional golf because their breasts got in the way and they spent more time struggling with their sexuality than lowering their handicaps. The writer's views were publicized widely and had a devastating effect on female athletes' acceptance in professional golf.

When *Playboy* magazine decided to feature gorgeous women who thrive in male-dominated sports like golf, Lisa teamed up with two other professional female athletes to prove that "women athletes can excel in men's sports and still be feminine." She decided to "show that sports writer"—literally! She and her colleagues appeared nude in a two-page, eight-picture photo spread in *Playboy*. In response to a flood of publicity and mixed perceptions, Lisa Ann said in her statement: "I hope people's perceptions are the same as they've always been—that I'm a highly confident woman who marches to her own drummer and isn't afraid to take a risk. Hopefully, I will inspire them to expand their horizons in some way."

Perhaps posing naked in a magazine seems a bit extreme to you as a response to unwanted or unwarranted rejection, but anger can be a powerful driving force, propelling you to leap hurdles you previously would have found too intimidating. Once the anger has dissipated, you might look back and wonder where you ever found the courage or chutzpah to do what you did.

While an "I'll show them attitude" often helps spark a new project or encourage a new direction, it has a downside if it becomes your sole motivator for the entire journey. Consider what Terri Bowersock went on to say about her experience at her high school reunion:

> The irony was that this motivation "to show them" pushed me for years, but when the moment finally came, it was rather unsatisfying. I looked around at my classmates and said to myself, "My God, I did all this for you?"
>
> If you're running a business for someone else, stop. Eventually, that becomes very shallow. No matter what you do, your own parents may never recognize it. Stop and do it for yourself, for your soul, for humanity. By the time I could flaunt my success to those who had made fun of me, their opinions didn't much matter anymore.

It is a wise person who knows how to take painful life experiences and turn rejection into motivation for success.

As Terri discovered, at some point your steam engine must be fueled by your own desires and deepest longings. Motivating yourself purely by reacting against outside forces can lead to burnout and an empty victory once you succeed. That said, until you identify and develop that inner desire, convert painful rejections into angry, resolute determination. Such a response makes the most of the lot life has given you.

 **TRY THIS!**

Consider to whom you still try to prove yourself. Is it your parents, a former teacher, your spouse, a business partner who left you for another opportunity, a former boss who fired you, a business coach or therapist who made you feel dysfunctional? All of us probably can identify at least one person who didn't believe in us, demeaned us in some way, or didn't see our potential. You may or may not be conscious of how much this person (or people) shaped your response to adversity now. Bless this naysayer for giving you the motivation to rise above your struggles. See the silver lining in his or her rejection of you at an earlier point in your life, for now it may ignite your entrepreneurial fires.

2. MOTIVATION: A MISSION GREATER THAN YOURSELF

The power of a mission greater than your own well-being will propel you out of your comfort zone. For example, you may be unwilling to go to the doctor for your own good, but you'll do it for the people who depend on you to stay healthy. Once you have gone public with your desire to succeed, whether it's via newspaper, television, radio, or word of mouth within your own family and community, you may exhibit courageous behavior that is uncharacteristic of you in order to avoid shaming or disappointing others. When you have teamed up with a group or partnership, you let not only yourself down if you fail—the entire group depends on you to do your part. That pressure is one advantage of not going solo.

Mission-based groups fight against all odds to achieve their goals because they so passionately believe in what they do. Terry Baker, cofounder of Chugwater Chili, from the tiny town of Chugwater, Wyoming, tells how she and her neighbors battled rejection when they united in a joint resolve:

> Our town of Chugwater, Wyoming, had 192 people in 1986. Just like lots of small towns in America, our town was dying. We lost our grocery store and bank. The restaurants were closing. Virtually all of the businesses were drying up and blowing away. Some of the newer people in town approached a few of us older folk to ask for our help to keep the town alive. The young folks hired a team to hold a forum for the townspeople, with the goal of starting an economic development group. At that meeting, we made a list of several ideas to keep Chugwater on the map. A resident of Chugwater was winning cookoffs with his chili recipe. Five of us couples got together, bought the recipe from him, trademarked the name, and we were in business!

> None of us had any background in finance, marketing, anything. The state gave us tons of help, all the newspapers picked us up, and suddenly we were celebrities on television and radio. People all around the state look at us as an example of what small towns can do. It was rough for many years, but we never let the constant rejection and hardships stop us. Over the last 11 years, slowly but surely, sometimes in spite of ourselves, we have built a successful business.

We couldn't possibly let all these people down. We all had a higher mission than just our own well-being or making money. We were fighting to keep our town alive.

Although most of us work for money, getting rich rarely works as a mission in and of itself. Rather, wealth and fame are the rewards of success when we follow our higher purposes and personal missions. Most of us want to contribute something meaningful to the world. When all you think about is making a sale, and you have lost touch with why you undertook your particular business in the first place, you will burn out and your work will cease being enjoyable. Even though you may be self-employed, you will feel like you have a job. The privilege of self-employment is that you can direct your energies passionately toward a higher purpose. If you lose that, you may as well work nine to five, collecting a steady paycheck and benefits.

Don't allow the work of your business and fatigue from its hardships to blind the vision you had when you first started. If you can't remember why you are in business, and your only purpose is to collect money at the end of the day, it may be time to search for another line of work. If you are employed in the right livelihood, fueled by a sense of purpose and fulfillment, you will be far more rejection-proof than if you work in a business that doesn't feed your soul. And if your livelihood is right for you, your higher power—guardian angels, God, or whatever universal force you believe in—will help guide you around any rejection-related obstacles in your way.

Consider this. What mission do you work for, beyond earning enough money to make yourself and your family comfortable? Is there anything or anyone who motivates you to push forward, even when the odds are against you and you feel discouraged? Do you believe that God has placed you on earth to do this work? Have you had a personal experience that makes you evangelistic about convincing others to receive the benefit of your product or services? Do you love someone or something enough to make you willing to bear rejection? These commitments may save you when you have one of those "quitting days."

 **TRY THIS!**

Regardless of your artistic ability, an easy way to create a visual image of your mission is to compile an affirmation collage. My artistic talent is limited to drawing stick figures, but I can cut pictures out of a magazine. I have done this exercise at four pivotal times in my life when I was making major life and career changes and needed extraordinary focus and encouragement.

Set aside a few hours, and gather a stack of magazines and newspapers lying around the house. Comb through these publications for pictures and words that represent the qualities you wish to have in your business, the higher purpose you feel you have on the planet, and what success will look and feel like for you and your loved ones once you achieve your business goals. Using a large piece of paper or cardboard, assemble these pictures and words into a collage and glue them in place.

Frame your collage and hang it on your office wall to inspire you to remember your greater vision when daily mundane worries take you off track.

3. MOTIVATION: FINANCIAL NEED

I have witnessed firsthand both the power and the powerlessness of financial need as a motivator for confronting the fear of rejection and inspiring a person to do what it takes to build a successful business. As I mentioned in the preface to this book, my husband, Stephen, was under a great deal of financial pressure when he began his accounting consultancy. We were supporting a large mortgage, student loans, three children, and a host of other expenses that demanded sizeable cash flow every month. My husband should have been highly motivated by our financial needs to pick up the phone and prospect for clients. Yet, for Stephen, these financial concerns still couldn't induce him to overcome his reluctance to cold call.

Fear of financial difficulty can paralyze you more than motivate you. Sales calls become too precious, every client too cherished, and the burden of financial obligations too heavy as you struggle to launch your business. A fine line exists between financial need that motivates you to action and financial need that makes you desperate, eats away at your self-esteem and confidence, and causes your effectiveness to decline.

Some of it depends on whether you are, by nature, an optimist or a pessimist. An optimist may be motivated by financial need because she believes that all will turn out for the good, so she doesn't allow her current money difficulties to trouble her too much. A pessimist may be traumatized by catastrophic thinking when financial troubles begin to cloud the picture.

For Joanna, a direct sales professional with three young children at home, financial obligations forced her to make a current situation work because the alternatives were intolerable:

> I was newly divorced, with no child support, and I had three babies, ages two through five, whom I was deter-

mined to keep out of daycare. Getting a job just wasn't an option for me. When my husband left us, I hadn't worked in five years outside of the house. I was using skin care products sold to me by a friend, with great results. The woman I bought the products from convinced me to take a stab at distributing the skin care products for a business. I have only a high school education, and I had never done sales before. I was scared to death when I first started. But every month, the rent had to be paid and the kids had to be fed. When I had trouble picking up the phone to call people, or if I started doubting myself, I'd just look at my kids and tell myself: "You have to do it for their sake." Now, one year later, my business brings me $3,000 each month, and I'm able to be home with my kids.

It helps to separate out your financial *needs* from your *wants* so you don't put undue pressure on yourself. If you are married, put together a family plan that details your business and household budgets, and determines what luxuries you will and will not do without while one or both of you are self-employed or earning volatile incomes. (Detailed instructions for how to create a family plan can be found in my book, *Honey, I Want to Start My Own Business: A Planning Guide for Couples.*)

Consider the difference between needing money to pay this month's rent and desiring enough extra cash to vacation in Hawaii. Financial need may backfire as a motivator when you try to take care of your basic survival and obligations, but it might work fabulously if your primary cash flow is covered and you aim to improve your lifestyle. Maybe that dream you've had for years to vacation in Hawaii is just the impetus you need to get yourself off the couch when you'd rather be napping!

TRY THIS!

When you work as an employee, you are compensated for your efforts every week with a paycheck. Most large sales organizations, life insurance companies, and network marketing companies reward their sales forces and their families with fabulous trips to exotic locations for reaching sales goals. I interviewed a father and son team for my book, *Let's Go Into Business Together: Eight Secrets for Successful Business Partnering,* who worked like gangbusters in their multilevel business to qualify for a trip they both wanted to enjoy. When the father was close to giving up on the ambitious task they had set for themselves, the trip motivated him to go the extra mile and the team qualified for the vacation.

If you are self-employed, working solo, borrow the wisdom of these companies and give yourself the same kind of reward package for working hard and surpassing your goals. First, pay yourself a salary every week. The amount doesn't matter; the act of payment does. If you are doing well enough to allow yourself some discretionary spending, set up a sales incentive system for yourself. For example, it might look something like any of the following options:

- When I earn my first $5,000, I will buy myself *[contact lenses].*
- When I get that consulting contract of $1,000 each month, and I receive my first payment, I will buy myself *[a new fax machine].*
- When I close at least ten new customers a week for three weeks in a row, I will buy my wife *[a dozen roses and dinner at a nice restaurant].*
- When I can deposit $5,000 into our savings account, I will take the kids to *[Disney World].*
- When my multilevel marketing business starts bringing me $500 each month in residual income, I will treat myself to *[a regular massage].*

Write down these goals, and post them somewhere in view during your working day. Make sure you deliver on your promises to yourself and your family unless urgent financial needs gobble up your money before it can go toward discretionary spending. Give yourself perks, just as a creative boss does to motivate a sales force, and your performance will rise to the occasion!

If you are a business owner with employees, consider offering your employees bonuses or special perks for helping you reach your goals. It is amazing how much more some employees are capable of achieving when they are offered more than a weekly paycheck as incentive.   ▪ ▪ ▪ ▪!

4. MOTIVATION: FEAR OF LOSING YOUR BUSINESS OR YOUR SALES JOB

Some business owners and salespeople perform best when under pressure. When they are in danger of losing their businesses or their sales positions, they rise to action. Until then, the pain of rejection is greater than the catalyst to push through the discomfort. The potential loss of livelihood, the shame of losing your business, or the thought of having to get a regular job can make you summon courage and determination you didn't even know you had!

Pam Lontos, the author of the foreword for this book, shared with me the pivotal moment in her career when she largely got over her fear of rejection:

> It was my first big sales job. I was working in health club sales. The owner of the health club, Jim, always yelled at me: "Don't say you can't do something unless you try. See that man putting groceries in his car? Go sell him." If I said, "Jim, I can't do that," he literally would push me out the door. I didn't want to lose my job, so I went. Jim

threw me out in the parking lot every day until selling was easy for me.

One day, it was raining and the owner couldn't send me out to the parking lot. There was no one in the club. He said, "You have to make your daily quota. Go sell someone. Go to North Park Bank." I went to the bank dressed in blue jeans, a leather jacket, and a T-shirt that said, "Do it every morning." Not exactly dressed for success! I couldn't go back to the club till I had sold someone. I was more afraid of Jim yelling at me than I was of being rejected.

When I saw all the no soliciting signs, I decided that if the bank president gave me permission to be there, I'd be okay. I asked a clerk where the president's office was. They assumed that I had an appointment. I took the elevator to his floor, and there was his secretary. I saw the nameplate "Tom" on his desk. I said, "I'm here to see Tom." Because I was dressed casually, she presumed I was a friend. She told me to go in his office. I planted myself in a chair and told him I was from the health club. I asked him whether he worked out, where he was hurting, etcetera. Maybe he was bored. Before you know it, he wrote me a check for $550 for a family membership for his wife and two teenage sons. Now he wanted to find someone to work out with. He took me through the whole bank, and I sold $5,000 worth of memberships that day.

I went back to the health club and handed the checks to Jim. He started laughing. He said, "Why would you choose *that* bank—the most prestigious bank in Dallas? I was only joking. That was the worst place to go!"

Pam chose between the lesser of two evils—confronting her fears of rejection or being yelled at by an angry boss who could fire her from a job she depended on. Nothing is wrong with forcing yourself to do the tasks you dread simply because you don't want to deal with the alternatives. Hopefully, over time, you will be motivated by more positive, upbeat inspiration, but when fear works as a motivator, terrific!

 **TRY THIS!**
■ ■ ■

When you need an extra kick in the pants, think of or write down ten phrases (examples follow) that complete this phrase: "I will do what it takes to succeed, even if I am uncomfortable being rejected. Rejection won't kill me, and it sure beats

1. getting a job."
2. shutting down my business."
3. laying off employees."
4. pulling my kids out of private school."
5. getting fired."
6. facing my wife if I don't make it."
7. wasting my dad's investment."
8. losing my savings."
9. destroying my credit rating."
10. not being able to pay the mortgage." ■ ■ ■ !

5. MOTIVATION: PERSONAL AND PROFESSIONAL GROWTH

Remember the metaphor I shared earlier in this chapter about how rejection can be like pests eating your garden? Rejection pests start out as an assortment of tiny creatures— maybe an infestation of bugs, a few mice, and small rabbits.

The problem with rejection is that the more you run away from it and allow it to terrify you, the bigger it becomes. Suddenly, those little critters become groundhogs and rabbits the size of small dogs, eating away at your garden so fast you don't know what hit you.

Letting rejection control you can make it impossible for you to ever achieve your dreams. If you run from rejection in one job or endeavor, it only rears up in your next one because rejection never disappears entirely, no matter what path you choose. The more you experience yourself as ineffective, the lower your self-esteem falls, until you convince yourself that you are no good at sales, or you are not suited to run a business. You can start believing that many opportunities are closed off for you because you fear rejection.

Some people—many who would buy a self-help book like this—decide that they will break through their phobia, even if it means they will be extremely uncomfortable for awhile, so that it won't ruin their careers. They recognize that their fears hold them back from their dreams. Because they are committed to personal growth and giving the most of themselves to the world, they obligate themselves to doing the deeper personal work it might require to transform fully how they respond to rejection. They might immerse themselves in the kind of training or job that is their worst nightmare—telemarketing, for example—because they see it as an opportunity to face their greatest fears and dissipate them. They might enroll in an intensive personal growth workshop or hire a personal coach who pushes them beyond their current limits. No pain, no gain for these folks, and they are willing to suffer to win the battle against the most serious obstacle to their success. For some people, the greatest motivation for getting a handle on rejection is to prevent rejection from getting a hold on them.

GOTCHA! WHEN REJECTION HURTS EVEN MORE

The stronger your motivation to succeed, the easier it is to withstand the pain of rejection. The opposite also is true: when your dedication to your business and passion about what you do are weak, rejection hurts even more. If, when a customer registers a complaint, you know that you've given the business your best and that the customer's gripe is preposterous, you can allow the criticism to roll off of your back more easily. If you have been careless, depressed, bored, working minimum hours, or failing to deliver the quality you know you are capable of, you will feel shame that the customer has caught you slacking off—especially if you normally have high standards for quality in your business.

It's the "gotcha!" syndrome. When you aren't working up to your own standards, you are more vulnerable to rejection and criticism because a part of you knows you deserve it. Keep your professional dedication and enthusiasm as high as possible. Maintain your standards of excellence, and never lose your commitment to success. That's how to build a fence high enough to keep those rejection pests from dining in your garden.

As we will discuss at length in Chapter 3, "Accept Your Limits," I don't believe that every entrepreneur or salesperson who desires to succeed can learn to handle all kinds of rejection, just because he is motivated and wants to succeed badly. That kind of motivational talk looks good on paper and sounds great in a speech, but most of us have limits we need to recognize and respect. While it helps to know what motivates you, it also is essential to respect what personal price you will and will not pay to succeed. Now let's take a closer look at this theory in the next chapter.

CHAPTER 3

Accept Your Limits, Then Stretch as Far as You Can

MAKING THE MOST OF WHAT YOU'VE GOT

I watched a moving story on the television magazine show "20/20" profiling a six-year-old girl who underwent the removal of half of her brain to stop constant and debilitating seizures. Doctors declared her paralyzed and dependent on a wheelchair for the rest of her life. They gave the girl's parents a gloomy prognosis for her mental and physical development, though the seizures finally stopped after this radical procedure. If the physicians had been right about their patient, this story would not have been of much interest to the "20/20" staff; thousands of people undergo brain surgery every day and face the same bleak prognoses. What landed this girl, now age 15, on prime time television was what she and her parents accomplished after the surgery. With thousands of hours of dedicated assistance from her parents over a period of years, constant physical therapy and tutoring (12 hours a day), extraordinary will, and the advice of a wise doctor at just the right time, this girl overcame her disability and joined her classmates in public school, where she excelled and earned straight "As." Not only did she lose her dependence on a wheelchair, but we witnessed her climbing a mountain at the end of the television segment.

Learning of this girl's remarkable recovery and the courage and determination she and her parents exhibited reminded me what human beings are capable of achieving when they put their minds to it and have the support systems they need. In fact, my bookshelves are stacked with motivational self-help resources that have reassured me, at critical junctures in my life, that I am capable of extraordinary achievement. Who doesn't feel reassured when reading classics like *Think and Grow Rich*, *How to Stop Worrying and Start Living*, and *The Power of Optimism*, which move us beyond the restrictions of our negative thinking and awaken us to the power we have to create magnificent success and prosperity.

LIMITS ARE OKAY

I do not argue with the inherent wisdom of teachers and authors who passionately assert that we are capable of anything we set our minds to, for it is true that we all are capable of extraordinary change and development. But let's face it: I would venture a guess that less than 5 percent of the world actually has the fortitude, dedication, and courage to surmount every obstacle that comes its way. The other 95 to 99 percent of us achieve moderate success given whatever weaknesses, fears, and laziness we carry with us as baggage.

I take a controversial position that differs from that promoted in most self-help motivational resources. I accept that you probably can't, or won't make some changes in this lifetime. When it comes to handling rejection and criticism in your business or job, you will never feel comfortable with certain situations and behaviors, no matter how much you dedicate yourself to improving your ability to surmount these challenges.

If the thought of cold calling makes you nauseous, you might never consider telemarketing as a career option. That's fine. If you ever choose to devote yourself to transforming your fear of cold calling, you might be an excellent telemarketer; however, nothing is wrong with realizing that this particular form of rejection is so abhorrent to you, you'd rather choose a career path that does not rely on cold calling to prospect clients. Instead of spending a great deal of time, energy, and money trying to be a master salesperson in all scenarios, choose instead the profession most conducive to your personality, then tackle with all of your being the obstacles that arise along that path. One lifelong salesperson shared the following thoughts with me:

> I found my sales niche was business-to-business consumables or service in which there is repeat business and the need to establish relationships. One-shot consumer sales were not my bag (for example, when I tried to sell cookware). However, I have friends who do very well at

one-shot sales but would be terrible at building relationships for repeat sales because they are irresponsible.

This chapter helps you determine your preferences and supports the growth you are capable of, with concrete steps you can take to improve your rejection resilience—within your comfort zone.

REJECTION AND CRITICISM COME IN DIFFERENT FORMS

In Chapter 1, we learned that the expression "fear of rejection" is misleading because what we really are afraid of is what underlies rejection, not the rejection itself. Another reason the expression is deceiving is this: More than likely, you do not fear rejection in all settings, but, rather, certain kinds of rejection trouble you, and others are not as big of a deal. Be careful of what you tell yourself. If you repeat the phrase "I can't handle rejection" often enough, you will come to believe that you cannot cope with any kind of rejection. I bet I can come up with an example that would roll right off your back.

The other day, I received a cold call from a telemarketer selling a meat service. She bragged about the quality of the company's meat, how far this quality surpassed supermarket brands. She didn't get far in her sales pitch when I told her we are an observant Jewish family and we buy only kosher meat. End of discussion—I have no use for her product. Do you think she felt rejected? Probably not. I wouldn't be a consumer of her product no matter how good it was or how effectively she presented her meat service.

Seasoned salespeople learn to adopt the attitude this salesperson shared with me:

I don't consider it a rejection, technically, if the prospect is not qualified—in other words, not a potential sale to begin with. In fact, if he is not a qualified prospect, he doesn't get a chance to reject *me;* I reject *him.* A kind of reverse rejection.

Not everyone, however, has developed such a positive attitude toward hearing the word *no* or being hung up on. Some folks—and maybe you are one of them—find *any* kind of rejection hard to swallow, even if it comes from an unqualified buyer. How rejection-sensitive are you?

 ## SELF-TEST: *WHERE ARE YOU THE MOST REJECTION-SENSITIVE?*

Listed below is a variety of situations in which you might encounter rejection and criticism as a business owner or salesperson. Even if a scenario doesn't apply to your current profession, imagine how you would feel handling the situation if you worked in a business where it did apply. In many of these situations, you may want to answer: "It depends." Of course, we can't capture the complexities of every business interaction in one sentence. For the purpose of this exercise, then, score yourself according to your gut reaction for the scenario you imagine being described.

Rate each scenario according to the following scale:

1. "I could care less. This kind of rejection or criticism wouldn't phase me in the least."

2. "This kind of rejection or criticism might sting a bit, but it wouldn't be a big deal."

3. "Rejection or criticism like this would hurt. I'd prefer not to experience it, but I could handle it."

4. "I would try my best to avoid this kind of rejection, but I would put myself in the situation if I had to."

5. "This kind of rejection or criticism would distress me so much I wouldn't put myself into a situation where it might occur."

■ ■ ■

1. Cold calling

____ by telephone strangers who have never heard of you or your product.

____ in person strangers who have never heard of you or your product.

____ by telephone warm leads referred to you by current customers or their friends.

____ in person warm leads referred to you by current customers or their friends.

2. Pitching your product or services by telephone to

____ close friends and family members.

____ neighbors, members of your synagogue or church, or other community organizations.

____ business acquaintances and colleagues.

3. Pitching your product or services by e-mail to

____ close friends and family members.

____ neighbors, members of your synagogue or church, or other community organizations.

____ business acquaintances and colleagues.

(continued)

4. You mail out 1,000 brochures for your product or services and get

___ a 30 percent response rate of interest (300 people).

___ a 5 percent response rate of interest (50 people).

___ no response of interest.

5. You provide information in person about your product or services.

___ A stranger says, "No thanks."

___ A friend or family member says, "No thanks."

___ A business acquaintance says, "No thanks."

6. The chamber of commerce asks you to offer a workshop to the community on your topic of expertise.

___ The chamber cancels the event due to lack of interest.

___ Ten out of 60 participants write on their evaluation forms that you were boring.

___ Five out of 60 participants walk out of your presentation in the middle of it.

___ The chamber director tells you that she wishes she had never hired you.

7. ___ As a network marketer, you start presenting your business opportunity to someone. Immediately, he says, "I don't want to have anything to do with a network marketing company. Forget it."

8. ___ Your product reflects hours of your artistic or creative work. When you present it to a prospective customer, she says, "This is really ugly. I don't like it at all."

9. You spend a full hour presenting your product or services to a qualified prospect. When you finish, he says

____ "I think your product is overpriced and cheaply made, and I can do better elsewhere."

____ "I like your product, but it's not in my budget right now. I will contact you if I ever decide that I wish to purchase something like this."

____ "I don't like dealing with a pushy salesperson. I don't like your style, and I won't buy anything from you. You are one of the worst salespersons I have ever heard."

10. Your work is reviewed publicly in some way—by book reviewers, a panel of judges, literary critics, movie reviewers, or professional associations, for example.

____ One negative review denigrates the quality of your work, though the rest of them are supremely positive.

____ More than half of the reviews are negative and denigrate the quality of your work. The rest are lukewarm or neutral.

11. ____ You are a chiropractor. At a social gathering, you hear someone say, "I think all chiropractors are quacks."

12. You are affiliated with a social organization to which you are committed passionately.

____ A current customer tells you that she won't continue to do business with you because she doesn't approve of your affiliation.

____ A prospective customer tells you that she won't consider doing business with you because she doesn't approve of your family's social affiliations.

13. ____ You are Jewish. You overhear a prospective customer in your store say, "I would never do business with anyone Jewish. They are so cheap, they would try to screw you."

(continued)

14. You decide to check out a professional networking event.

   ___ You discover that the group is very cliquish, and no one is friendly or cordial to you as a new guest.

   ___ You connect immediately with a few members who are very friendly, but by the end of the evening, no one has expressed much interest in your product or services.

15. A sizeable percentage of your current customers start buying your product elsewhere. They tell you it is because

   ___ your prices are too high.

   ___ your product or services are no longer state of the art or competitive, and the quality is poor.

   ___ they don't like an employee of yours.

   ___ they don't like you.

16. One of your oldest customers complains about your services. When you don't resolve the dispute to his liking, he tells you he will no longer do business with you. His business represents a(n)

   ___ significant portion of your cash flow.

   ___ insignificant portion of your cash flow.

17. An irate customer shouts insults and vulgarities at you.

   ___ Her business represents a significant portion of your cash flow.

   ___ Her business represents an insignificant portion of your cash flow.

   ___ The customer is a family member or close friend, and the relationship is very important to you.

   ___ The customer is a business colleague who sits on your professional association's board of directors.

18. You distribute a free online newsletter via the Internet. When a stranger requests that you remove him from the list of subscribers, he sends the message:

    ____ "Please unsubscribe me from your newsletter. I don't need this kind of information anymore."

    ____ "Take me off of the list of subscribers immediately. I don't need any more junk mail."

    ____ "I found this issue to be very poorly written and in-accurate. I normally enjoy your newsletter very much, so I was disappointed in you."

    ____ Subscribers requesting to be taken off the list increase daily, although you don't know why. They have given no explanations.

19. A national publisher releases the first book you have written.

    ____ You organize a book signing at a bookstore in your home town, and only four people show up.

    ____ You are invited to a book signing at a bookstore in another state, and only four people show up.

    ____ You are invited to be a guest on a nationally syndicated radio program that is heard in more than 200 locations. A caller attacks you for your point of view and says your book is lousy.

    ____ You are invited to be a guest on the AM radio station heard in your home town. You've lined up all of your family and friends to listen. A caller attacks you for your point of view and says your book is lousy.

...?

EVALUATING YOUR SCORES

This self-test has no right or wrong answers. How you score is less important than how that score matches the profession you want to succeed in. If you are a life insurance salesperson and prospecting strangers is key to your business success, you are in trouble if you rated all of the cold calling questions a "5." If you run a retail store, you may have no problem if you rated cold calling a "5," but if you have a meltdown when a customer complains for any reason, you could find that profession entirely too painful.

Take a look first at all of your "5s." Unless you are incredibly determined, experience some radical shift in your psyche, undergo hypnosis, or connect to a phenomenal trainer or coach, these are rejection phobias you are unlikely to change significantly in your lifetime. These fears and resistances are rooted deeply in core beliefs you've developed since childhood, traumatic experiences you've never recovered from, and behaviors that go entirely against the grain of your personality. To shift these from a "5" to a "3" or "4," you can try throwing yourself fully into the activities you dread often enough that they lose their emotional charge and become no big deal—a desensitization process. This strategy works for a small percentage of people, however.

Despite the odds, many professionals plan to desensitize themselves to their phobias. You might even hire a sales trainer to push you to undertake the activities you currently find impossible. Still, for the "5s" on your list, you usually find ways to procrastinate or prohibit yourself from engaging in business activities you find too agonizing, even with a sales trainer or supervisor trying to motivate you. You may spend an inordinate amount of time planning and learning to undertake these activities without actually accomplishing them. Maybe your motivation to succeed is so strong you will do virtually anything to succeed, despite your rejection phobias. If you are one of those people who will let nothing stand in your way, even if it means facing the "5s" on your list, go for it!

Today, as I was writing this chapter, I took a break to purchase a car telephone. The man who waited on me at the retail store had a severe stutter. I was impressed that he would place himself in such a customer-intensive environment when talking obviously was a tremendous challenge for him. I could only imagine the rejection he has suffered in his life and how he has learned to cope. By choosing retail sales as his profession, apparently he had either become so rejection-proof that reaction to his stutter didn't phase him anymore or he was not letting his stutter hold him back from what he wanted to do. Although our interaction took twice as long as it might have with another salesperson, any inconvenience was replaced by admiration for his courage.

Most of us are average human beings, capable of achieving great things and modifying some personal behavior, but nothing quite so revolutionary as reversing powerful phobias. We are better off giving our attention to those aspects of our personalities that we most likely can change and choosing professions in which we are most apt to succeed. Some of us will never telemarket, sell to family members, have our work reviewed publicly, speak in front of large groups, or handle regular complaints in a customer-intensive business. *If you choose a profession that requires mastering circumstances you currently rate a "5," you probably will waste a lot of time and money trying to fix yourself, with poor results.*

Now review your "1s" and "2s." Congratulations! Here is evidence that you can handle rejection in all kinds of circumstances. If you carry the notion that rejection is always difficult for you, remember that it probably is painful only *in certain situations.* Once you discover what those conditions are, you can either choose a profession that doesn't require you to face your strongest fears or work on improving your responses to those difficulties you rate "3s" or "4s."

Now examine your "3s" and "4s." Here is your greatest chance for significant progress toward becoming rejection-proof. By using the tools and techniques you'll learn in this book, perhaps seeking additional sales training and personal coaching, and undertaking the activities so often they become routine, over time you can convert these scores to "1s," "2s," and "3s."

ACCEPT AND WORK AROUND YOUR LIMITS

Reflexively, you might have a problem with the concept of accepting and working around your limits. After all, it won't get you very far if you let your weaknesses rule, right? We are trained to ignore, hide, be ashamed of, and deny our deficiencies, as if it is possible for any human being to be exceptional in all endeavors, at any hour of the day.

One of the secrets to building your rejection defenses is to acknowledge when and how you operate at less than full capacity, then to work around it. Following are some examples of how to honor your less-than-optimal abilities without giving in to them fully and allowing them to destroy your business.

Make the Most of Your Circadian Rhythm

Dr. Tony Alessandra, best-selling business book author and sales trainer, advises you to know your circadian rhythms— that is, the ebb and flow of your energy during the day. Are you a morning person or a night owl? Determine when you usually operate at peak effectiveness so that you can orga-

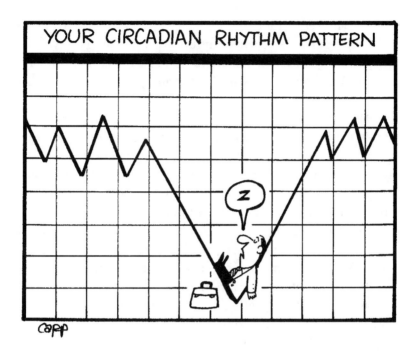

nize your sales activity to capitalize on that energy. If you are at your best after lunch, making sales presentations first thing in the morning may not be a good idea. On the other hand, if you tend to need an afternoon nap and lose your energy by 3 PM, putting off your sales activity until late in the afternoon is not the best way to organize your work day.

When your verbal energy is low, that's the ideal time to take care of paperwork, planning, written communication, and other business details that don't demand the same level of charismatic energy. This recommendation conflicts with some sales training programs that suggest you should always plan your sales calls for first thing in the morning, in order to get them over with, so that you can move on with the rest of your day. Hilton Johnson, sales trainer, warns:

The reason for making sales calls in the morning is that regardless of whether you are a morning or evening person, you're more likely to do it. At the end of the day, you have too many wheels spinning.

Also, if you procrastinate sales calls until day-end because they are frightening for you, you might have to force yourself to make them in the morning, whether that's in sync with your circadian rhythm or not, just to be sure that you do them. In that case, you'll need to find ways to energize yourself before the calls, if you aren't normally "up" in the beginning of the day. If you try to do any activity that is challenging when you are low in energy, it's like putting rocks in your backpack while climbing a mountain.

As a professional, you must learn to perform when duty calls, regardless of whether you are fatigued or preoccupied with other matters. When you have a choice, it's a good idea to plan your day around when you know you are typically at your best and worst.

Only Commit to Those Activities That You Will Actually Do

For example, say you decide that you want to write a best-selling book. With 60,000 new books released every year, it takes a lot more than a great book to land on the bestseller list these days. Books sell millions of copies when the authors promote those books 16 to 20 hours a day. The *Chicken Soup For the Soul* books have sold over 25 million copies, not just because they are great books, but because the coauthors are tireless promoters. Jack Canfield and Mark Victor-Hansen do on average one media interview a day, every day, year after year. Although it might sound great to say to yourself and others, "I want to write a bestseller," before you set your sights on such a lofty goal, you must ask yourself how many hours and resources you are willing to commit in order to make that happen.

Mark Good, owner and sales trainer for the Sandler Business Institute in Lancaster, Pennsylvania, recommends to his clients that they limit their sales activity to what they are capable of committing to do. If you are having difficulty with cold calling, and your current ability is to just pick up the phone and call one person, do that. Make yourself accountable to someone—it can be your spouse or your child who says: "Dad, did you make your ten calls today?," or it can be a mentor, coach, or sales trainer. The key is knowing what you can emotionally handle, and then *committing* to that. Mark tells this amusing story from his early days in sales, before he became rejection-proof:

> Because I loved golf, I started selling a handicapping system to golf courses. But I couldn't sell. My boss requested that I do forty cold calls a day. I couldn't handle that. I made a deal with him that I would dial the phone twenty times. He agreed that I could stop dialing the phone as soon as I had twenty dials, even if no one answered. And I could stop cold calling entirely once I had two appointments.
>
> I remember coming into the office at 6 AM to call businesses, because I knew they wouldn't be open. I would dial my twenty calls and speak to no one. Once I called a company in Arizona—at 3 AM their time, and a guy answered the phone. I figured he was the janitor. Who else would answer at that time? I told him I was surprised to get an answer, and he said: " I'm always here." I asked him if he was the janitor. "No," he replied. "I'm the president of the company."

"You won't believe this," I said. "I was hoping to reach you!" I explained to him who I was, and made my pitch. He wasn't interested.

Accidents happen and someone picks up the phone every once in awhile. Eventually I became comfortable enough with the process that I was able to make more appointments and become more effective.

If you are terrified of approaching strangers, and haven't spoken to a stranger by phone or in person about your business in the past month, it is entirely unrealistic for you to set a goal that, "starting Monday," you will make 20 cold calls a day, or that you will go to three networking events a week. Although it's admirable that you desire to succeed, it is unlikely that you will make the necessary changes overnight. Just ask the millions of dieters in this country who dream of losing 20 pounds in a month, starting on Monday morning. By Tuesday, most have returned to their old eating habits, hoping that next Monday they will summon the willpower to try again.

Set small goals that you can realistically commit to and accomplish; maybe it's making one cold call during the following week, or contacting a warm business contact that you've had in your rolodex for a while. If you'd like to increase your attendance at community functions, make a phone call to the local chamber of commerce and ask for membership information as a first step. If going to networking functions isn't a problem for you, but you have a tendency to only hang out with the people you already know once you get there, set a goal that at the next event, you will introduce yourself to one new person.

Let go of the illusion that you can transform from timid to self-confident by just wanting it bad enough. Start with where you are, and allow incremental progress to be good enough. As you experience success and your self-assurance naturally grows, you will gradually increase your tolerance for rejection, and be able to pursue and succeed at more ambitious goals.

Chunking It Down

When you give yourself permission to start with where you are, take your big dreams and long-range goals and break them down into smaller, doable steps. I first heard the expression "chunk it down" many years ago in a personal growth workshop, and I've seen it from time to time in magazines and books I've read since then. It always refers to setting reasonable goals that you can accomplish in a given day, or week, or month.

Each time I see a contract from my publisher for a 70–80,000 word book, I feel overwhelmed. Early in the process I always wonder how I will get it done. So I set up a schedule for myself, and determine how many words I need to write every day, in order to finish a certain number of chapters per month, so that I will complete the book on schedule. When I realize that it is within my abilities to write 1000 words a day, I relax. You can do the same with virtually any business activity in which you engage. Break it down into daily, even hourly activities, and give yourself regular doses of positive reinforcement as you progress toward your bigger goals.

 **TRY THIS!**

Goal Setting from Where You Are

Identify your biggest sales challenge. It can be related to contacting the prospect, making the sales presentation, talking in front of a group of people, showing your work to interested buyers, finishing a piece of work that will be subject to evaluation and review, and so on. Answer these questions for the challenge you selected:

1. What do you want to achieve in three to six months?
2. What are you willing to do every month to reach that goal?
3. What are you willing to do every week to reach your first monthly goal? Your second monthly goal? Your third? And so on.
4. What are you willing to do every day to reach your first weekly goal? Your second weekly goal? Your third? And so on.
5. Are you willing to commit to the daily activity required to achieve your three-month to six-month goal? If not, rewrite your goal until you arrive at one that requires daily activity you are willing to commit to.
6. What will you do today?

Whenever you feel overwhelmed by the magnitude of something you are trying to achieve, break it down. Focus on what you can do today or right now to move you closer to where you want to be. All those days add up, and before you know it, you are hitting your target. ∎∎∎!

Spouse as Advocate or Adversary

Accepting your limitations and stretching beyond them is easier when you have support from family, friends, and colleagues who want the best for you. In *Honey, I Want to Start My Own Business: A Planning Guide for Couples* I discuss in depth the impact that a supportive—or an unsupportive—spouse has on a struggling entrepreneur.

Your spouse can make your life easier by taking care of household and family responsibilities to free up your time for the business. She can hug you and lend moral support when your spirits are low. He can help you as an adviser, an employee, or a partner in your business. She can remind you of your talent and how much she believes in you when you question your abilities and whether you should remain committed to your business.

Your spouse also may be angry that you aren't making enough money, as well as judgmental of your limitations. He may pressure you to quit your job or close your business when you have a rough time making it work. You fall off of your pedestal quickly when your wife sees you quiver in fear because you have to pick up the phone and call a prospect, when you receive the first big criticism of your work that she agrees with, or you create considerable financial stress for your family when you are ineffective in your business. When your spouse is affected by your sour or distracted mood and volatile cash flow but feels powerless to do anything about it, he might tell you how to do your job better. This strategy often backfires and creates tension in a marriage.

If your relationship strains under the pressures of business difficulties, try some of the strategies I suggest in *Honey, I Want to Start My Own Business,* and seek professional help from a marriage counselor or business coach who specializes in assisting entrepreneurial couples.

Turning to Colleagues for Support

Laura Douglas, a marketing analyst, shared this strategy for making her hard days in sales a bit easier:

> If I am beating down doors cold calling for a day, the next day I make sure I see clients who want to see me. I go to see the clients who think of me as their daughter, or flirt with me, or like to talk opera with me—the people

who make me feel good because they like to see me. If I am dealing with some kind of personal rejection, I spend time with people who think I'm wonderful—Internet acquaintances, members of the chamber of commerce, committees where I volunteer my time. I've created places to go to feed my soul when I need to lick my wounds.

You, too, can join professional organizations and give of your time in your industry so that you can turn to the people you get to know when you need professional feedback. If you require professional training, enroll in a sales seminar or attend conferences where you can meet peers who are in your business, struggling with the same concerns that you are.

Hiring a Sales Coach

If personal selling is the key to your business success and you need to improve, consider hiring a sales coach or getting some comprehensive sales training during your career. If you hire a sales coach, interview him privately about his experiences. If he only brags to you about how sales comes naturally to him and he's never had any problem with rejection, find another coach. Masterful salespeople usually are not professionals who never have had a problem selling but rather people who have worked through enormous obstacles to get where they are. You will find some recommended resources for sales training at the back of this book.

Nancy Stephens, a sales trainer from Carlisle, Massachusetts, and author of *Customer-Focused Selling*, cautions:

> Forget the myth of the natural-born salesperson. It isn't true. And it's a myth that's destroyed a lot of sales careers.

I've known a lot of salespeople, and I've yet to meet a person who's confided in me that he or she was an absolute, instant smash hit in selling! Instead, I constantly meet lots of really successful salespeople who tell me the same story—of how they built their sales abilities over long periods of time, combining both skill building and practice.

Hire a personal or business coach with whom you can talk by telephone or in person for a period of months, someone who will be your cheerleader and mentor but hold you accountable and kick you in the butt when you need prompting. A sales coach can help you overcome rejection and grow personally in the process of selling yourself and your services or product. This relationship can be extremely valuable if you find the right coach. A business partner, mentor, or sales manager also can fulfill the role.

Look for a coach who supports you and has high regard for you but also pushes you—gently—to a new level. If a sales coach makes you feel bad about yourself as a way to motivate you to improve, run—don't walk—away from that relationship. Few people benefit from paying another person a lot of money to make them feel worse about themselves. Honor your intuition and end the relationship promptly if it doesn't serve you.

When you meet colleagues you admire, ask them whether they have ever worked with a coach whom they would recommend. This can be your best way of locating someone to assist you. Don't hesitate to interview several coaches until you find someone who feels right.

You may not have the money for a personal coach, or you might not wish to spend your resources on such assistance at this time. Instead, consider attending a sales training workshop offered locally or nationwide. Because you have so many to choose from, ask for referrals from business colleagues you trust. Attend the workshop of a known master in the field, or buy the series of cassette tapes she produces. Hundreds of master sales trainers have written books you can purchase in your local bookstore.

You will find lots of resources available in printed and online magazines, newsletters, chat rooms, news groups, chapter meetings, and regional and annual conventions if you are involved in a national network marketing company or another national firm that offers training. Take seriously your commitment to improving your salesmanship and personal effectiveness, and be sure to designate a portion of your profits or investment to ongoing professional training. Superstars never stop learning and pushing their limits.

CHAPTER 4

Tame Your Mind

THE POWER OF THE UNCONSCIOUS MIND

Getting a handle on your fear of rejection and your sensitivity to criticism is an inside job. The problem begins in your mind, and the solution resides there, too. The power of your conscious and unconscious mind is awesome. That's both good and bad news. You can drive yourself crazy with your worries and inhibitions, but you also can set yourself free. Because rejection and criticism always accompany you on your entrepreneurial journey, the best you can hope to do is minimize their occurrence and their ability to cause you distress. The most successful among us aren't those who have escaped rejection but those who have harnessed their minds to focus energy in a positive direction, rather than being trapped in depression, defensiveness, and fear.

The most stunning illustration of the power of the mind over behavior I have ever seen occurred in May of 1998 when I watched a CBS television special called "Hypnotized." The show featured a world-class hypnotist who showcased his incredible talents by hypnotizing volunteers in everyday settings with their peers present, then, through the hypnotist's power of suggestion, leading the subjects to undertake an assortment of wild, crazy, and humorous activities. Throughout this program, I saw lessons for the rejection-terrified.

In one episode, the hypnotist convinced a woman sunning at the beach that a beachball weighed 500 pounds and that she was incapable of picking it up, let alone throwing it. When he brought her out of her trance, unaware of his decree, she agreed to toss the beachball around with several partners. To her utter dismay, whenever she received the beachball, she crashed into the sand, unable to bear its monstrous weight. She couldn't understand why that same ball seemed lightweight to others because to her it weighed 500 pounds. The hypnotist's trance was so powerful, the woman's subconscious mind believed the beachball was too heavy to carry; thus, to her it was.

If you are terrified of being rejected, picking up the telephone to prospect for clients feels like the phone weighs 500 pounds. As the phobia increases and negative repercussions occur from lack of effective sales calls, the phone starts weighing more and more, until you develop creative excuses never to lift the phone at all. Like the woman on the beach, you believe the phone is too heavy to pick up, no matter what the objective reality.

The hypnotist went on to convince others that doors were locked that weren't—even that doors existed that didn't. My husband and I watched in amazement as a man who had been hypnotized fought violently to get out of a dressing room in a men's clothing store, pounding on a door that didn't exist as a group of astonished customers looked on. One unsuspecting man who had been hypnotized similarly went to buy a pack of gum in a convenience store, not realizing that the hypnotist had convinced him that his hand would get stuck in his pocket while reaching for change. None of his efforts or those of other customers would free his hand from his pants pocket.

If you lack self-confidence, all barriers in your business appear to be as real as the invisible door that the clothing customer banged against. In a trance of your own making, you convince yourself of impediments too formidable to overcome, even though some barriers exist only in your imagination. Perhaps you tell yourself that no one wants to buy beauty products from an overweight person or your lack of formal education will make others think you are stupid. Although in some settings these obstacles may be valid impediments to success, a determined salesperson with the right mind-set stampedes right over the hurdles.

In one of the television program's most outrageous scenes, the hypnotist visited a barbershop and placed a few customers under hypnosis. He then implanted in each subconscious the suggestion that when the barber told the customer his haircut was finished, the customer would see himself as entirely bald when he looked in the mirror. Meanwhile, the barber actually had not cut the customer's hair or even touched his head at all. Sure enough, my husband and I watched, incredulous, as each man freaked out about what he saw—an entirely bald head—even though the physical evidence was to the contrary. In the men's clothing store, the hypnotist even convinced one customer that when he looked in the mirror to appraise a new suit, he was naked. The man screamed in horror upon looking in the lobby mirror and seeing himself naked in front of a group of other customers—even though he was fully clothed in a brand new suit.

If you suffer from low self-esteem, the image in the mirror does at times appear "bald" or "naked," and you are convinced your vulnerability is obvious and exposed to all around you. The professional speaker worries that the audience will realize that he doesn't have a clue what he's talking about and he will be "undressed" at the podium. The businesswoman who takes great pains to beautify herself before attending a critical networking meeting fears that everyone in the room will view her as a frumpy lady in a thrift store suit trying to act like a grown-up. Every businessperson fears, at some time in his career, being undressed in front of his customers and peers and being exposed as an imposter.

The power of the subconscious mind, as the hypnotist demonstrated, also holds good news for business professionals. Just as we may be convinced of obstacles and detriments that aren't really there, the mind can so convince us of success that we act as if it is true. For example, the hypnotist convinced willing bowlers that they finally would bowl the perfect "300" game—strikes every time. The catch is he also set up the suggestion so that in reality these bowlers actually would throw a gutter bowl each time. No matter. Each time the bowlers threw their balls, everyone watching in the bowling alley saw gutter balls. The bowlers, however, saw perfect strikes, and they jumped up and down in ecstasy upon experiencing their phenomenal skill.

The hypnotist also induced a woman shopping in a pet store who confessed to a phobia of snakes to believe that she adored snakes as much as puppies and kittens. The pet store staff placed a huge python in her lap, and within minutes the woman was caressing the snake and kissing it on the head as if it were a cherished golden retriever puppy.

Many of you feel the same way about making sales calls as you do about caressing a giant python. Yet if you could approach sales, networking, and customer service with excitement and joy, you would set up a self-fulfilling prophecy: Your sales would escalate, and then selling *would* be enjoyable! Next time you approach a new client, can you imagine him or her to be an adorable golden retriever puppy? Better not—you might break out into uncontrollable laughter. On second thought, worse things could happen.

In this chapter, we will focus on training our minds to do what we wish we could hire a hypnotist to do for us—shift our thoughts and deeds into positive, success-producing activity.

THE NUMBERS GAME—DETACHMENT

When I interviewed more than 120 professional salespeople and business owners for this book, certain themes started repeating themselves. This was one of them: Make a game of the noes, seeing them only as tickets to the inevitable yeses. Without a gamelike strategy, depression and hopelessness quickly take over. The businessperson starts making excuses for not prospecting, and the downward cycle begins. No calls, no appointments, no sales.

No human being can withstand an onslaught of constant and regular rejection unless the person can detach from it and view it as a means to an end.

Ken Knouse, a master salesperson and author of *True Prosperity: Your Guide to a Cash-Based Lifestyle,* told me this story about the critical moment early in his career when he really "got" this concept:

I needed a job. The previous Friday, I had quit my second sales job in eight months. The position in question [that I was ready to interview for] paid straight commission. It was the only game in town, and I was ready to play. It was better than nothing. The regional sales manager pitched me, using his visual aid—a ring binder with plastic page protectors. When he explained the commission structure and the compensation plan, he changed my whole perspective on selling. He explained the numbers game.

He said if I made 20 sales calls each day, I would average two presentations per day and would sell one out of four presentations, one deal every other day. This wasn't speculation, he said. This was a matter of fact. The company had kept records. Twenty calls, four presentations, one sale. With an average of 22 work days [each month], I would sell 11 deals a month. At an average commission of $100 per sale, I could expect to make $1,100 per month. The regional sales manager closed by saying, "If we hire you, we will expect you to make 20 calls every day. Does this sound like something you can do?"

I knew what he wanted. He wanted a believer. "I *know* I can," I declared. I made a commitment. He hooked me.

That afternoon and evening, I memorized the presentation, using the ring binder with the plastic page protectors. The next day, I began making calls. Four weeks straight, I made 20 calls each day. At the end of the month, I had ten sales, more than a thousand dollars in commission, the most money I had ever made. I averaged ten-plus sales per month until I became branch sales manager.

Selling, which had seemed such an intimidating and complicated process, suddenly became ridiculously simple. All I had to do was make 20 calls each day and wham, the sales appeared. No longer did it matter what happened on an individual call or whether the prospect bought or not. All that mattered was that I made that call plus 19 others. The calls were just numbers. There was no success or failure, only numbers. Selling became a numbers game, and the pursuit of numbers became fun.

In the past, fear of failure had kept me from making enough calls to be successful because to my previous supervisors, if a prospect didn't buy, I had failed. My supervisors scrutinized every call that didn't result in a sale, pointing out my mistakes. If only I had done this or that, then I would have sold the deal.

Let's face it. Most calls don't result in sales, no matter how good the salesperson is. I was miserable; I hated failing. So I did the only sensible thing—I cut my losses by keeping my calls to a minimum. No calls, no sales.

The numbers game changed all of this. Now I was eager to make calls, even though I knew that most of the time I would get a no. It didn't matter. The important thing was to get a decision from the customer because a decision—it didn't matter if it was positive or negative—

validated the call and my efforts. Now, a no actually made me happy. It put me one step closer to a sale.

Hilton Johnson, a sales trainer, credits a mentor and fellow sales trainer, Tom Hopkings, for an expression he teaches coaching clients to say to themselves when they prospect and they hear a no: "Thanks for the $20!"

Hilton explains:

> Let's say that the total commission you make on an average sale is $2,000. How many presentations do you have to give to get that? How many appointments do you have to set to give that many presentations? Let's say it usually takes 100 calls to get enough appointments and presentations to make one sale. That means each call is worth $20! So every time you dial the phone, even if the person doesn't answer at all or hangs up on you, say to yourself, "Thanks for the $20," because if you keep making those calls, you'll eventually get the $2,000.

CONVERT CONCERN TO CURIOSITY

As a syndicated columnist and author, I have gotten used to waiting a long time before getting an answer—often no—when I try to sell my work to a publishing house, magazine, or newspaper. If you make your living in any profession where a long lead time occurs between when you make your pitch and when you know whether you've made a sale, you understand what that waiting period is like. At first, you are wildly optimistic that you will hear back rapidly, even though that isn't very realistic, because you expect the prospect to be so enthralled with your work she doesn't want to let you get away. After a few weeks pass, you let go of that fantasy and become hopeful that the prospect will read your materials and decide favorably. Something happens after about four weeks. Fading optimism is replaced by pessimistic thoughts: "Maybe no news is bad news. He probably isn't interested." Or "The editor (or whoever) is so busy, I bet she never even opened my mail." As the weeks roll along, pessimism can move to fatalism: "I don't know why I want to make a living in this crazy business anyway. I should go get a job!" Or "Who am I kidding? I must not be any good. They would have called by now."

 **TRY THIS!**

In the business you are in, if waiting and worrying are the norm, you can't do much about the waiting period, which reflects the industry. What you can learn to do something about is the worrying. Here are a few tips:

1. Convert concern to curiosity by changing your mental dialogue in the absence of feedback. When you begin to tell yourself something negative, stop and replace it with a more positive statement that also could be true:

- "I know it feels like a long wait to me, but in this business waiting one month is nothing."
- "I bet they are busy and haven't had a chance to look at my material yet. I still believe they will love it when they see it."
- "The universe always provides me with what I need. If this isn't the answer, something better will come along."

On a piece of paper or in your journal, write down three negative statements you often tell yourself when you have made a presentation and are waiting to see whether the prospect is interested in what you have to offer. Now replace them with three positive statements that you could tell yourself instead.

2. Keep yourself busy in the interim. Even one week feels like an eternity if you wait for the phone to ring and do not engage in other activities that will help you prosper and keep your mind active. Don't let yourself fall into the trap of not leaving the house or office because you don't want to miss a phone call or postponing new business activity because you tell yourself, "I'll just wait to see whether I get this gig before I start pursuing anything new." When you are involved in many projects, waiting for one to finalize, no matter how important it is to you, is easier.

3. Follow up with a phone call. In a vacuum, your mind fills in what it imagines is happening, which may be far from the truth. Just this morning, I called a newspaper editor I had sent samples of my column to more than a month ago. I was feeling pessimistic, assuming lack of interest on his part. When I reached him, he said quite casually, while munching on his lunch, "Yeah, I got your stuff. Haven't looked at it yet; been too busy. I will look at it though, and I'll call you when I do." He still might not buy my column, but now I can move the conversation in my head from pessimistic to hopeful again by making that quick phone call.

You probably avoid making such a phone call because you are afraid of being rejected. It's easier to send your brochures, proposals, cassette tapes, or whatever in the mail and wait for the phone to ring. Think of it this way: You already tell yourself something bad, so it can't get much worse! Last week, I forced myself to call a busy magazine editor to follow up on a query I had sent. I was nervous and shy about interrupting her; I was very conscious of how many people must call her every day, and I didn't want to be a pest. The conversation lasted only a minute. She let me know that she was under a tight deadline getting the current issue out, and she wouldn't be looking at my query for a few weeks. If she was interested, she would call me. At least I knew where I stood and that it could be awhile before I heard, and she knew I was committed to the project. ...!

Mark Nelson, an independent distributor for the network marketing company FORMOR International, told me that the tape system, (sending cassette tapes by mail to people on mailing lists and responding to interested callers rather than cold calling people on the telephone) isn't working very well. The system works best when distributors follow up with phone calls, but most representatives are too petrified of calling to do that. Mark sees multilevel marketers wasting thousands of dollars on cassette tapes because they won't make follow-up phone calls.

It's more painful to hear rejection over the telephone than to simply interpret a lack of response as lack of interest, but professionals in just about every industry agree that following up after you've forwarded your materials for consideration is important if you want to improve your acceptance rate. (In some cases you are prohibited from following up. I recently entered a writing contest, and the rules stated: "No phone calls; send SASE and we'll let you know." Most of the time, though, rules don't prohibit you from calling; your timidity does. Remember this: The longer you delay making that phone call, the harder it becomes as you move along the spectrum from optimistic and hopeful to pessimistic and convinced that you are a loser and no one wants to buy your product. Practice sales techniques designed to reduce resistance to help make those calls less painful. Make the calls when you feel confident that the prospects would be lucky to be your customers.

THREE STRATEGIES FOR MANAGING FEAR

Don't wait until you find a way to eliminate fear. Even the most experienced and successful salespersons experience some fear as they do what it takes to work their business. If you are going to learn to "feel the fear and do it anyway," here are three strategies to consider for reducing your stress level.

1. FEAR (False Expectations Appearing Real)

Many years ago, I heard the expression "FEAR stands for **F**alse **E**vidence **A**ppearing **R**eal." Over the years, I've changed it to an acronym that has more meaning for me: **F**alse **E**xpectations **A**ppearing **R**eal. When you expect disaster, you often get it. When you worry about your deficiencies and believe that they will prohibit you from being successful, lo and behold, they do. You set up a self-fulfilling prophecy because your fear diminishes your effectiveness; thus, your confidence wanes, and you are less convincing the next time you try to sell.

A powerful way to master fear is to spell out your worst fears in the most minute detail. That's right, actually write down your worst nightmare. When you do this, you probably will see how unlikely it is that your deepest fears will come true. An example follows:

- *I am afraid that . . .* I won't be able to bring in enough business this month.
- *And if this happens, I am afraid that . . .* I will go bankrupt within a few months.
- *And if this happens, I am afraid that . . .* we will lose our house, my wife will leave me, and my kids will despise me as a total failure.
- *And if this happens, I am afraid that . . .* I'll kill myself because I couldn't face myself or others.

If this is what you fear, every rejection will feel like a death sentence.

You can learn to replace negative thoughts with positive affirmations:

- *Even if I don't get this sale* . . . we'll never lose the house because my mom and dad would help us out if I had to ask.
- *Even if my business doesn't make it* . . . I can find a job. I know I'm employable.
- *Even if I don't get this sale* . . . I know that my wife won't leave me. We have a solid marriage, and she loves me, whether or not my business prospers.

 **TRY THIS!**
■ ■ ■

1. Write down your worst fears in as much detail as you can. Write as many sentences as it takes to reach the truth about what you are ultimately afraid of. You can use the space provided here, or better yet use another piece of paper with more room to get as specific as possible. Then create positive affirmations to counteract the FEAR (false expectations appearing real). If you keep working at building your business and don't let your fear paralyze you from action, you may come to realize that the positive scenarios are more likely to occur than the ones you fear.

_____

_____

_____

_____

_____

2. Find out exactly why you didn't make the sale. You also may experience false expectations about why you didn't close a sale. In the absence of clear communication, your imagination fills in the blanks with what you believe is the reason you were rejected—and it could be far from the truth. What you imagine may be a whole lot worse than the reality.   **....!**

Jeff Tobe, a dynamic professional speaker from Pittsburgh, Pennsylvania, has heard plenty of rejection in his career because the professional speaking industry is extremely competitive. He advises:

> Over the span of many years, I have learned that the reason I am not hired for a particular event often is not personal at all but related more to the size of the client's budget or political issues, like someone in the company recommended another speaker. I always ask why I am not being hired when a prospective client says no. What I learn usually makes me feel better, not worse, about being rejected because often I cannot control the rejection and it is not personal at all.

And what if the feedback *is* personal? You must make room for customer preferences and choices. You may not be what a customer is looking for at the moment, no matter how good you are. If you hold a false expectation that you will make every sale you aim for, please every customer, and never experience rejection, you surely will be disappointed. Every customer rejection is feedback for you. Rejection isn't the enemy but rather a guiding mentor that improves your performance if you pay attention to what it teaches you.

2. *"What If"*

Another way to look at the false expectations and fears that fill your mind is to examine the "what-ifs" that keep you up at night or make you sick to your stomach right before making a presentation or pitching yourself to a potential client. I am well aware of the power of what-if talk. In July of 1997, I discovered that I was pregnant with our third child. As we would soon have three babies younger than age four, as well as two teenage sons from my husband's previous marriage, I was—to put it mildly—overwhelmed by the news. My worst moments occurred at 4 AM, when my worries about how we would manage kept me wide awake, staring at the ceiling and obsessing about the what-ifs.

- What if the baby wasn't healthy?
- What if I had a difficult pregnancy and was bedridden with two toddlers in the house?
- What if I threw up from morning sickness on the podium during one of my speaking engagements?
- What if my husband was laid off and we lost our medical benefits?

The list of catastrophic what-ifs was endless. I shared some of my darkest fears with a colleague, Robin Silverman, who recently had survived the floods of 1997 that wiped out her town of Grand Forks, North Dakota. Having faced great tragedy and come through a stronger, happier person, she was a wellspring of support and advice for me. She sent me this e-mail one morning:

Az—
Just for fun, here are a few what-ifs you might not be considering right now.

- What if this child discovers the cure for cancer?
- What if he/she has the sweetest smile this side of heaven?
- What if he/she turns out to rescue one of your other children—emotionally, physically, or financially—in an hour of need?
- What if he/she is the President of the United States in 2052?
- What if he/she teaches you a life lesson you'd never learn any other way?
- What if this whole thing turns out to be a lot more fun than you probably think it's going to be?

Bingo! Robin was absolutely right. Because what-ifs were only a product of my imagination, I might as well use the time to imagine positive thoughts instead of negative ones. What would I have to lose, except my fear?

Perhaps you face your fear of rejection as you prepare for a client presentation or wait for a prospective client to get back to you on whether you've been hired for a project you really want. Your thoughts may run as follows:

- What will I do if the prospect doesn't want to buy my product or service? How about: What if I land the most lucrative contract I've ever received?
- What if the prospect doesn't like my work and she tells all her friends how awful I was? How about: What if the prospect loves my work and refers me to all her friends?
- What if I go out of business because I don't make enough income this year? How about: What if I land a big deal during the next year?

When negative what-if thoughts bombard you, train your mind to shift to a positive opposite. Think of some of your worse nightmares, then find positive replacements. Allow your imagination to soar. What-ifs are composed in your head anyway, so you might as well treat yourself to some great fantasies.

TRY THIS!

Write down the top five what-if fears that enter your mind when you are about to make a sales call or deliver your product or service to a client or an audience who will evaluate you. Then write down five positive what-ifs that you can say to yourself instead.

3. Where's the Proof?

Melissa Blair, founder of Sales Concepts, Inc., is the kind of sales trainer you want to have. She overcame extraordinary resistance to selling early in her career and has great empathy for her struggling clients. One formative early selling experience almost stopped her from ever selling again:

My first sales job, at the age of 25 was at a weight-loss clinic. My job was to take interested prospects on a tour of the clinic and sign them up for our services. On my first day, the manager of the clinic quit and I was left to run the clinic myself. I had eight people signed up to come in for the tour. I did not close on the first seven. Panicked, I knew I had to close the last one or be laughed out of the job. So when the woman gave me the standard objection, "I have to ask my husband before I spend this much money," I pushed and pushed until I got her to give in.

The following morning, she returned to the clinic. She had a black eye and bruises on her face. Her husband beat her because she had spent the money. She was crying and begging me to return her money. The policy at that time was to label it buyer's remorse and attempt to resell her on the program. I couldn't do that. I quickly returned her money, and it became a companywide joke about how I had lost eight consultations out of eight.

I went on to manage two of their weight-loss centers, but I never overcame my hesitancy to sell. I always preferred the task-oriented aspects of management instead of the sales. It got so bad that when we were given lists of phone numbers of former clients to resolicit, I would mark them as deceased or relocated rather than actually make the phone calls. Didn't I set a great example for my staff?

A few years later, when Melissa joined her mother in a partnership to offer sales training, she encountered the groundbreaking work of George Dudley and Shannon Goodson, authors of *Earning What You Are Worth*. She wasn't planning to do any sales in the new business; she was responsible for bookkeeping and the administrative side of things. Melissa went on to tell me:

> My mom and I needed only one phone in our office because she quickly learned that I was never going to use it! Then I learned from George and Shannon that I could take control of my thoughts and challenge my old beliefs about my ability to sell by asking myself three questions:
>
> 1. Where's the proof that this has to be a frightening situation?
> 2. Do I have to feel the fear I'm feeling right now? Does the situation require me to feel it?

3. Even if I believe that I have to feel the fear I am feeling, and even if I cannot feel any other way, do I have to feel my fear as much as I feel it now?

Because I now take the time to evaluate each situation logically, I am able to take control and change my behavior. I no longer let my thoughts mindlessly dictate my actions. Most importantly, as my results changed, so did my self-esteem. I was able to get to the point where my thoughts about my ability to sell changed into positive ones.

JUST DO IT! TAKE ACTION

Action and victories do more to change your negative self-talk and low self-image than mental gymnastics ever can. The primary purpose of the mind-shift exercises we've discussed so far is to get you to take action. Confidence in yourself and your services builds with every new satisfied client and every praise of your work. When you shift your self-fulfilling prophecy to expect success, fear of rejection subsides as you become convinced that anyone would be lucky to do business with you, and whoever passes on the opportunity is the loser, not you.

Even though you may have trouble with the rejection factor in cold calling, this sales representative takes a "just do it!" attitude that works for him:

Whenever I get negative about the potential for growth in my business, I get out and make calls—lots of cold calls. The wealth of opportunity becomes apparent to me, and I'm cured of my negativity.

LIGHTEN UP

You purchased this book because you take your career seriously and you want more success in your life. Getting what you want is serious business—it takes focused effort, skill, and training. Most people won't reach their potential because they aren't dedicated or willing to suffer enough. Ironically, it also helps if you don't take your business and yourself too seriously. There is a time to work hard and a time to let go. Sometimes the best way to handle your fears and sensitivities is to laugh at yourself and stop caring so much—lighten up!

If you were to experience a tragedy in your life, or in the life of someone close to you, you probably would put it all in perspective and realize that worrying about each dollar you earn or sale you make is relatively meaningless in the total context of life. When you give birth or say good-bye to a dying loved one, you don't think about your bank account. When you hear that a good friend's house has just burned down, you get outside of yourself and think about how to help your friend. The facts of your business haven't changed—you still need to make sales and please a certain number of people to prosper in your business. But for the time being, your mind focuses on other, more important things. You are yanked out of your self-absorption and worries, and for a few hours or days it is easier to keep business in perspective—until the crisis passes and your life resumes normalcy.

Therefore, take yourself seriously, but not too seriously, and be sure to give of yourself and have fun in activities outside of your business. Spend time cavorting with your kids or watching them play Little League softball. Cuddle up to your spouse, and give him a back rub. Volunteer at your church picnic. Take a break in the middle of the day to see a matinee. Sometimes you are better off ignoring your worries than confronting them. Distract yourself and focus your attention on giving of yourself to someone in need. When you get your mind off of your troubles and help someone else, you have the opportunity to put your business needs and concerns into perspective and to realize that perfecting your next sales call would be marvelous, but it's not essential to creating a joyful, meaningful life.

VISUALIZING SUCCESS

Olympic athletes have a way to train themselves to be their best that has nothing to do with physical exertion or athletic skill. With only seconds, or sometimes hundredths of seconds, separating those who win medals from those who don't, the difference often lies in an athlete's brain, not in her body. Every world-class athlete has worked just as hard mastering the use of his imagination and positive visualization to give him the winning edge as he has perfecting his athletic performance. The winning athlete has pictured thousands of times, in great detail, how it feels to win the race. When she goes out to do it on the big day, it's like deja vu because she's been there so many times before. Mary Lou Retton, the Olympic gymnast, was asked what she was thinking as she started down the runway to a perfect "10" on the horse. "Watch this!" she said.

I read about a groundbreaking experiment that proves the power of positive visualization for athletic performance. Members of a basketball team were divided into three groups. One group practiced free throws in the gym for 20 minutes a day for a month. The second group never entered the gym; each player spent 20 minutes a day visualizing himself making perfect free throws. The control group neither practiced nor visualized. At the end of the month, the group that practiced in the gym had improved its free-throw average by 24 percent. The group that visualized itself making free throws improved by 23 percent. The third group showed no improvement. *Virtually no difference existed between the influence of visualization and actual practice!* To the subconscious mind, practicing in your head is the same as practicing with your body.

Now imagine that you are an Olympic salesperson. You are preparing for the big games in the year 2000, when salespeople from all over the globe will assemble to compete against each other to prove who is the greatest salesperson in the world. (Or imagine an Olympic competition in your field, as the best professionals in your industry gather to compete for the gold medal.)

As you prepare for the Olympics, you might visualize all the bad things that can happen if you aren't in top form. We call that worry. Worry is nothing more than negative visualization. You already know how to visualize if you can see your failures and your what-ifs in vivid detail. Perhaps you've gone over in your head dozens of times how it feels to have a prospect hang up the phone on you, a customer criticize you, or an audience member walk out of one of your presentations. All you need to do is train your mind to convert your negative visualizations to positive ones.

Visualize yourself receiving the gold medal at the Olympic games. Imagine how millions of people admire your abilities as you step onto the podium to receive your medal. Feel the gold medal pressing against your chest and the self-respect you experience as you are recognized the world over for your mastery of sales and customer service in your profession. Imagine the standing ovation you receive from your customers and peers. You are now so rejection-proof that criticism bounces off of you without wounding you anymore. Customers clamor for your product or services. You project self-confidence, and your reputation for excellence is respected around the world. Your loving spouse, family, and friends are with you, watching you receive your award and swelling with pride. It's your fantasy—make it anything you wish!

Before you pick up the telephone or leave the house to engage in any kind of sales activity, rehearse a positive outcome in your mind. To help you reach a state of calm, rely on a phrase or prayer that is meaningful for you. Choose a passage from the Bible or a favorite book, or make one up yourself. Many years ago, I wrote the following poem, which I put to a melody. Whenever I am anxious before a speaking engagement, I sing this poem as I get dressed and prepare for the day. I have sung it so many thousands of times, just humming the melody often calms me. You may borrow this prayer, but I encourage you to make up one of your own:

Please, Lord, watch over me today,
For only one thing I hope and I pray.
May I have the courage to get out of the way,
And allow Your wisdom to guide my day.

May I follow my heart, where I know You reside,
and when I hear Your voice, may I always abide.

In complete faith, I surrender my fear,
knowing that You are always near.

Replace your negative thoughts with positive affirmations and your worries with prayer, and as sure as night follows day you will experierence prosperity, achievement, and inner peace.

Develop Your Flexibility and Resiliency Muscles

YOU CAN DEVELOP FLEXIBILITY
AND RESILIENCY

Develop flexibility and resiliency if you wish to thrive as a self-employed professional or salesperson. Flexibility is the ability to roll with the punches, to respond to what *is* instead of what you want it to be. Being flexible means that you accept the possibility that you don't always have the right answer and that circumstances always are, in some way, perfect just as they are, even if you do not understand how at the time. When you are flexible, you let go of your rigidity and desire for control and allow yourself to change course when you must. *Flexibility is a loosening of your posture and attitude.*

Resiliency is an anchoring of your posture and attitude. It's the refusal to let anyone or anything stop you from achieving your dreams. It's getting angry or determined when someone tells you that something can't be done. It's your ability to overcome obstacles and to push forward with renewed determination and courage, even when you've experienced a challenge to your business success. You are resilient if you can bounce back quickly from disappointment and accept a certain amount of rejection instead of letting it flatten you.

No matter how detailed and thorough your business plan, how skilled your sales presentation, or how much in demand your product or services, you will encounter unpredictable disappointments and obstacles that don't fit your perception of the perfect plan. This chapter is designed to help you adapt to the detours, winding roads, and stop signs you encounter as you travel the road of self-employment. Imagine that you can exercise every day at the health club to develop your resiliency and flexibility muscles. Following are six work-out strategies.

1. BELIEVE THAT WHATEVER IS, IS FOR THE BEST

Although losing a particular sale or favored client may seem like a major disappointment at the time, it could turn out to be the best thing that happens to you. The following parable demonstrates a basic truth about life: You won't know whether a life event is positive or negative until the end of your days, when you see how everything turns out.

One day, a poor farmer's son returned home with a fine stallion. His neighbors gathered around to congratulate the farmer on his good fortune. "How do you know this is good fortune?" the farmer asked. Several weeks later, the horse ran away to the land of the barbarians. When the neighbors expressed their condolences, he asked "How do you know this is bad luck?" Months later the stallion returned with a herd of fine mares, and the neighbors again were delighted with his good luck, but he asked "How do you know this isn't a catastrophe?" Sure enough, as his son was breaking the wild horses, he fell and shattered his leg. When the neighbors expressed their sympathy the farmer said, "Who says this is a misfortune?" The next month, the Emperor declared war on a neighboring kingdom and conscripted all the able-bodied young men of the village. Nine-tenths of them never returned from the war. (From the *Huai Nan Tzu*)

Optimistic and successful people find a way to frame every life experience as a positive one, regardless of how it appears at the time. They believe that when one door closes, another opens, so they always open new doors (or, depending on their faith, believe that God opens the doors for them).

Let's consider three basic ways to respond to a disappointment or a change of direction in your business. Which group do you fall into?

1. Victim. You know you've become acquainted with people in the first category if you avoid asking them the simple question "How are you?" You'd like to be friendly or helpful, but you always get an earful about how horrible everything is in their lives, how none of it is their fault, and how it's all unfair. They are intent on feeling sorry for themselves and gaining your sympathy. If they have lost important sales, the prospects were idiots. If valued employees quit, it's impossible to keep good people these days. If their businesses start to fail, they list all kinds of reasons, none of them because of deficits in their skills. You avoid victims because it's such a downer to converse with them and there's no such thing as a quick conversation. Once they have a captive audience, they won't let you go; listening to them is like being strangled.

Victims learn little from their rejection experiences because they insist that none of the rejection was their fault. They grow bitter and angry and are unlikely to prosper in sales or small business for very long. Their customers and family avoid them because they don't want to listen to the victims' tales of misery. If they experience some bad luck or a particularly difficult rejection, as we all do, victims fail to make something positive come from it. They lose their businesses, or their businesses don't grow prosperously. Years later, they still are angry at the people they blame for their losses. Victims live in the past, dwelling on what could have been, if only.

Jeff, a former independent bookstore owner, still is resentful of how the chain bookstores—Barnes & Noble and Borders—gobbled up his customers, taking away his market share and forcing him to close his store. Five years later, he works temporary jobs and lives month to month in a rented apartment. He's stuck—too angry and frightened to run his own business again and unwilling to commit to any new profession as an employee. He still mourns the loss of his business and has been unable to build a new, satisfying life since losing it.

Probably you aren't a victim or you wouldn't have bought this book. Victims rarely take responsibility for improving their skills or life experience.

2. Blessings in hindsight. The second group of people find blessings in business disappointments—but only in hindsight. They grumble and complain throughout the entire unwelcome experience, cursing their bad luck and wishing things could be different. Once the difficulties have passed, however, they often recast the way they perceive the events, conceding that it's the best thing that ever happened to them—but only when they discover something positive has come from it.

The following story, written by Michael Angier for the online newsletter *Success Digest* (www.successnet.org), typifies such a group of people:

> What makes Enterprise, Alabama, especially memorable is a strange monument they have in the middle of town. You can't miss it. In fact, you have to drive around it because it sits right in the middle of the road. The monument is a statue to the boll weevil.
>
> It's probably the only monument in the world erected in honor of an insect. It certainly wasn't done because of its aesthetic value—the boll weevil is a particularly ugly-looking creature. Surprisingly, it was erected because of the devastation the boll weevil caused to the cotton crops of the surrounding area!

Why did they honor this pest? Well, had it not been for the boll weevil, the local economy would have continued its unhealthy dependence on its one-crop, one-product economy. Until then, everything depended entirely on cotton. When the boll weevil came, the farmers and all the other businesses that were reliant on the cotton farmers were forced to recognize the need to diversify.

In the long run, they saw that the boll weevil had, in fact, done them a favor by destroying their crops. No longer were their eggs all in one "cotton basket." They started raising hogs, peanuts, and other cash crops, and the entire area was better off for it.

I would guess that you fall into the second category most of the time. You *can* see the silver lining in the clouds but not until the storm subsides, the dust settles, and you are on your feet again. You need time to regroup, whine, sulk, cry, and scream when something important doesn't go your way. You have a basic belief that all will turn out okay, but you can lose faith in God and yourself and become quite depressed or immobilized when you experience a disappointment in your business. Eventually, you pick yourself up and focus on new beginnings, and when something positive develops, you retrospectively bless the setback you once cursed.

Maggie, a real estate broker who specializes in selling real estate to high-income individuals, understands the roller coaster of real estate sales, so she doesn't spend her commission checks until she deposits them in her bank account. She still remembers one of her most difficult blows—losing a million dollar home at the last minute because the buyer was fired from his executive position a day before the closing. Maggie considered leaving real estate after that one—for about two days. Then she forced herself right back into the game. She never did sell that house. However, two years

later, the buyer who had pulled out of the deal was successfully reemployed, and he remembered how gracious Maggie
had been when he suffered his loss. He contacted Maggie and
purchased a $2 million estate through her firm. "Never burn
a bridge," Maggie preaches.

As I have become more rejection-proof over the years, the
amount of time I allow myself to rant or despair becomes
shorter and shorter. These days, I rarely worry about any
business disappointment for more than a few hours or days
at the most because I am so confident that everything that
happens is meant to be, and it will all turn out fine in the
end. I have had enough experience losing something I cov-
eted, only to find that something even better fills in the gap.
When I'm in a positive frame of mind and lose a business opportunity I was hoping for, I immediately become curious
about what will arrive in its place. The universe abhors a
vacuum; something new and often better always shows up.

3. Immediate acceptance. *Gam zu Letovah,* Hebrew
for "this, too, is for the best," is your motto if you fall into
this third category. You start looking for the rainbow as soon
as the clouds appear. Your faith in God or a higher power is
so strong that you surrender yourself completely to doing
His or Her will, and you are genuinely satisfied with whatever shows up, figuring that it's all meant to be. You are so
optimistic and self-confident that you approach rejection
like a game. You are curious when something doesn't go your
way, wondering what the rejection is telling you about your
journey and where you'll go next. When you ask someone in
this third category how she is doing, you may hear about her
troubles, but most often you hear about her faith and what
she is doing to solve any problems. Nine times out of ten, before the conversation is over, she asks you how you are doing
because she doesn't see the universe revolving around her-

self. You know whether you have ever met anyone in this category. You marvel at the person's strength, courage, and eternal faith and optimism.

Sharon is the president of a multimillion dollar Internet-based retail organization. She has unwavering faith, which gives her extraordinary flexibility and resiliency:

> I believe that I am on this earth to serve Jesus Christ, my savior. He has granted me all of the success I have achieved, and I am His servant. When I don't get something I want, I figure that He knows best, and it's not something I'm supposed to have. I wait for Him to show me the right way. I pray every morning before I start my day that His will be done. When I get stuck, I turn it over to Him and ask for guidance. At the end of every day, I thank Him for any success I've achieved. It makes my life very simple and peaceful. I don't worry about rejection anymore because I know that He's in charge.

Perhaps you've thought to yourself: "Thank goodness God doesn't give me everything I wanted because I got something much better instead." My husband, Stephen, was distressed about the loss of his first marriage because he was categorically against the idea of divorce. Our marriage, however, is much more satisfying to him than was his former. It's a good thing he didn't get what he wanted.

 **TRY THIS!**
■ ■ ■

Here's a fun exercise to help you shift from whining over what you didn't get to appreciating the benefits that may come instead. Do this gratitude exercise to help you see how much good has resulted in your life from *not* getting what you wanted. For example, one business owner, a literary agent, shared with me: "I'm so grateful that I didn't get any of the jobs I wanted when I was interviewing for them. The people who said no to me did me a big favor because now I'm doing the kind of creative work I never would have imagined."

To begin, think about how you would fill in these blanks:

I am so grateful that _____, even though I wasn't happy about it at the time. This disappointment lead me to _____, and as a result, I _____, which is better than it would have been if I hadn't been forced to try something new.

For example:

I am so grateful that I lost my biggest client, even though I wasn't happy about it at the time. This disappointment led me to expand my services in new ways, and as a result, I increased my sales by 20 percent, which is better than it would have been if I hadn't been forced to try something new.

Or

I am so grateful that my bookkeeper resigned for another job, even though I wasn't happy about it at the time. This disappointment led me to learn how to handle the bookkeeping myself for a period of time, and as a result, I got a better handle on where all of my money is going and I reduced operating expenses by 20 percent, which is better than it would have been if I hadn't been forced to try something new.

Now go back and repeat this exercise a few more times. Eventually, it will become second nature for you to think this way when you feel disappointed.   ...!

Develop an attitude of gratitude and optimism in the face of whatever initially unwelcome circumstances you encounter. This is the finest strategy I know of for increasing your resiliency and flexibility muscles.

2. ALLOW YOURSELF TIME TO MOURN
IF YOU NEED IT

I advocated in the first section of this chapter to look for the positive in whatever comes your way and to be grateful for where it leads you. Even so, you may need to grieve before you can accept fully a severe blow to your business or self-esteem. Grieving often can't be rushed; you'll likely move through denial, anger, depression, then, finally, acceptance at your own pace. Rejection that is hardest to handle usually falls in the category of personal betrayal, devastating financial loss, or loss of a life-long dream (like giving up on getting a work published after multiple rejections).

In response to adversity of this magnitude, you may decide to switch professions, get a new job, close down your business, or radically change the way you do business. Perhaps you'll move through the grieving cycle in a week, a month, or a year or two. Whatever it takes, your business may suffer or even slow to a standstill. You may take time off until you feel more solid, then come back with renewed energy and determination.

The following three professionals dealt with their grief in very different ways when they experienced rejections in their businesses. Each needed to go through the process he or she went through to emerge productive and healed. There is no one right way to grieve a business loss.

Rick, the owner of a dating service in the Midwest, enjoyed a relatively quick recovery:

I started a dating service with a friend of mine. We were having a great time and making lots of money. Out of the blue one day, he announced to me that he wanted to start a new business with his wife. We'd either have to sell the business, or I'd have to buy out his half. First, I tried to convince him that he could do both businesses, but then I got really mad. I felt abandoned, and I was furious that he sprung this on me with no warning.

My anger lasted a few days, but it faded as I focused on finding the cash to buy him out. When I figured out a way to make it work and presented a buyout proposal to him, he accepted it, and within a few weeks I was solo. I didn't allow myself much time to get upset because I had to stay focused on running the business. It took me a year or so to forgive my friend for pulling out on me. Now, the business is doing great, and I enjoy being able to run it on my own. It was for the best, after all.

On the other hand, recovery can take months, even years. Michael Angier is founder and publisher of *SuccessNetworks, International*, an organization located in South Burlington, Vermont. It took Michael a few years to rebound from a particularly devastating rejection:

In my previous business, I owned a four-color glossy magazine with the largest circulation in Vermont. I had a devoted staff of nine. We had just finished a retreat where everyone was saying things to me such as: "This is the best company I've ever worked for. My relationship with you is the finest I've ever had with any employer."

Six weeks later, at the end of 1990, the local economy crashed. Practically overnight, we went from five checks a day in the mail to five days with no checks. Customers stopped paying their bills—and I was the last in line. We were highly leveraged, so when cash stopped flowing in, I was out of business. I had to lay off my staff. It was crushing.

When I told my staff the bad news, they heaped all kinds of outraged judgments on me, accusing me of ruining the company and their careers.

I went from hero to zero in six weeks. But I was the same guy!

It took a year and a half to feel like myself again. Receiving that level of rejection and animosity, plus losing my business, destroyed my self-confidence and self-esteem. I was so identified with my company I took everyone's rejection to heart.

Michael went on to create an entirely new venture that gives him great satisfaction, but he couldn't have done that within days of losing his company and being attacked by his former staff. He wasn't ready until he had regained his self-esteem and detached himself from the rejection that he allowed to stop him. Michael couldn't accomplish this feat in just a few days or weeks. It required almost two years and the support of Michael's family and closest friends.

Barbara is a former mystery writer who suffered the loss of her dream and the need to change course:

I spent two years writing my novel, but I couldn't find a literary agent to represent me. I tried to sell the book myself, but I collected a big pile of rejection letters. I remember the day an agent called and took the time to give me some honest feedback instead of just sending me a form letter. She encouraged me to find another profession and to keep writing as a hobby!

I was devastated. Being a published author was a lifelong dream. But I listened to her because I had received no positive feedback on my novel, so maybe she was right.

I began working for a friend in her retail store. I grew to like the work. Now, I write just for fun, and I don't worry about getting published. I enjoy writing again— and that's more important to me than getting published! I may have lost the dream of seeing my name on the front cover of a book, but at least I didn't lose the joy that writing gives me.

Barbara spent most of her grieving in the depression cycle, gradually moving into acceptance. She didn't need to accept the verdict of the agent who contacted her. If she had gotten angry, perhaps she would have fought back by taking some writing classes, getting some professional coaching, or continuing her search for the right publisher or another agent. Instead, she chose to remove herself from the profession that was giving her so much grief, and she came to peace with her decision.

3. FIND PEOPLE AND ACTIVITIES TO SUPPORT YOUR SOUL DURING DIFFICULT TIMES

Developing flexibility and resiliency is always easier when loving people in your life support you and believe in your value and the contribution you can make. Although it's ideal to boost your own self-esteem, most of us benefit tremendously from outside encouragement. Your spouse, children, parents, close friends, or business colleagues may be sources of great comfort and inspiration when you feel particularly down-trodden or need extra motivation to rebound from adverse circumstances.

Whatever your occupation, join a membership organiza-tion or an Internet discussion group that puts you in regu-lar contact with others in your profession. For example, I am on several Internet mailing lists for authors and publishers and a long-time member of the National Speakers Associ-ation. As an active participant in these organizations, I read and listen to the experiences of other writers and speakers, learn creative ways to respond to common problems, and, most of all, find moral support.

Develop a relationship with a business colleague you can vent to—someone who will listen, empathize, and help you find solutions. A person you see regularly over lunch or cof-fee or a cyberspace buddy with whom you exchange e-mail may be your support. Such relationships are priceless for self-employed professionals. Remember that to receive from these relationships, you must be willing to give, so take time to offer advice and encouragement to others if you wish to receive it from them.

Also develop support systems outside of work with peo-ple who love you whether or not you are a successful profes-sional. One close friend or a loving spouse can do wonders to help you stay focused and optimistic when your business challenges you. This may be someone you pour your heart out to or ask advice of or even someone who helps you get your mind off of your business.

Sometimes rebounding doesn't mean fighting back but rather getting away from the problem until you sort out how to handle it or come up with a new approach. If you are a workaholic with no life outside of your job, you'll find it difficult to get the psychological break you might need to be more creative. Make room in your life for activities that nurture your soul and give you joy. Engage in a hobby, spend time with your children, volunteer in your community, exercise at a health club, or participate in a sports league. David, a computer consultant who regularly works long hours, shares:

> I play volleyball every Tuesday night with a group of buddies. We all work in different professions, and we rarely talk about work when we're together. I don't want to spend my time off complaining about my job. I want to have a good time and get my mind off work for a few hours.

If work takes all of your time and energy, when your business is in upheaval or you wait for an important deal to close, your emotional state will be driven completely by your business circumstances. Develop a full life that extends beyond your work, and you'll find it much easier to stay calm when business is volatile.

In a university commencement address several years ago, Brian Dyson, CEO of Coca Cola Enterprises, spoke of the relation of work to one's other commitments:

> Imagine life as a game in which you are juggling some five balls in the air. You name them work, family, health, friends, and spirit, and you're keeping all of these in the air. You will soon understand that work is a rubber ball. If you drop it, it will bounce back. But the other four balls—family, health, friends, and spirit—are made of glass. If you drop one of these, it will be irrevocably scuffed, marked, nicked, damaged, or even shattered. They will never be the same. You must understand that and strive for balance in your life.

 **TRY THIS!**
■ ■ ■

Think of three people or activities to which you would like to devote more time, and determine what you must do to accomplish that. For example: "I'd like to get back to painting. I need to buy myself some art supplies and allow myself a few hours on weekends to relax and paint." Write these things down and post the paper somewhere, like the refrigerator or bathroom mirror, to give you a constant reminder of your goals.   ■■■!

Have any of the four glass balls Brian Dyson refers to—family, health, friends, and spirit—already shattered because you have dropped them too often? Commit today to reenergize those aspects of your life that are undeveloped or suffer from neglect. If you want people to be there for you in difficult times, you must spend time developing those relationships when you do not need their support. If you want to strengthen your flexibility and resiliency, nurture your soul.

4. LET HISTORY ENLIGHTEN AND REASSURE YOU

You don't develop resiliency overnight—it's a lifetime in the making. As an adult, the more hurdles you overcome and difficult experiences you endure, the stronger you should be in the face of new challenges. It's not uncommon for business owners to fail in a variety of professional ventures before learning from their mistakes and becoming successful.

Reflect on your childhood and adult experiences. Think of two or three major accomplishments you have achieved that took a great deal of courage, commitment, skill, and persistence. Here are some examples:

- Getting into the college of your choice or graduating with honors from college
- Dealing with a difficult boss in your previous job
- Performing in a music or dance competition as a child
- Enduring a divorce, serious illness, or loss of an intimate family member

From the time you entered the world, you began strengthening your resiliency and flexibility muscles. My toddlers must learn alternatives to screaming and crying when they don't get something they want. My teenage stepsons have developed more sophisticated methods for acting out when they are unhappy with house rules; more often, they bargain or reluctantly do what it takes to get what they want. Accepting and responding to the reality that you don't always get what you want, how you want it, when you want it is one of life's great lessons. If you continue to indulge in tantrums as an adult, you will remain a victim your entire life.

Look back over the events of your life that required flexibility and resilience. What helped you get through these difficult times? What skills and strengths did you develop that will help you now, as you master challenges in your work? When you were under great pressure in the past, what did you rely on (your faith? family? inner drive?) to keep you motivated and on track?

History can be your best reassurance that you have the strength, courage, and character to survive a current ordeal, just as you have others in the past. Loved ones and your higher power will remind you of your strength when you have forgotten. Don't reinvent the wheel if you don't have to. Look for clues in your past to determine what you must rely on now when you are tested.

5. RESPOND CREATIVELY TO OBSTACLES AND PROBLEMS

A lesson from the American West teaches how facing problems or challenges head on can be lifesaving. In freezing rains, heavy snows, or below-zero temperatures, most cattle turn their backs to the icy blasts and move downwind until they come up against a barbed wire fence. In big storms, many cattle pile up against the fence and die. Herefords survive consistently, however, because in a storm they head into the wind, stand shoulder to shoulder, heads down, and face the blasts.

Entrepreneurs who face life's storms head on develop not only their flexibility and resiliency muscles, but their creativity muscles as well. They think outside of the box and look for solutions that may not be easy or right in front of them to salvage a deal, keep a customer happy, or entice a reluctant prospect to buy. They don't run from difficulty; rather, they face it head on and seek solutions. The funniest, most creative example I have seen of an imaginative response to potential disaster is that of Jeff Slutsky, a professional speaker who shares this hilarious story in many of his keynote addresses and in *Chicken Soup for the Soul at Work.* Here is his story, shared with his permission in its entirety:

Nothing is more important to the success of a business than satisfied clients. Satisfied clients stay with you and refer their friends to you. Plus, keeping an existing client costs you a fraction of what it takes to bring a new client to replace a dissatisfied one that has left. The single biggest reason clients leave is broken promises. The single most important rule for keeping your clients is: "When you make a promise, either stated or implied, do your best to keep it, regardless of the cost."

I was home in Columbus, Ohio, sound asleep. It was 2 AM, and I was awakened by a phone call: one of my clients. I was scheduled to give a presentation in Marco Island, Florida, later that same morning at 9 AM, and I was supposed to have arrived the night before. Panic set in. For some reason, I thought the program was in two days.

How did this happen? It didn't matter. The immediate problem was a speech that had to be done in several hours, and I was a thousand miles away with no conceivable way to get there.

I frantically started looking through the yellow pages for charter planes. I called six or seven, but no one was answering at two in the morning. Finally one did. It was an air ambulance service. The guy asked me what the emergency was. I told him that if I wasn't in Marco Island by 7 AM that morning, my client was going to kill me. I asked if they could do it. He responded by asking me if I had an American Express card. As I quoted my Corporate Card number over the phone, he assured me there was no problem. Their Lear jet ambulance would have me there by 7 AM.

I called the client back and told him that I had chartered, at my own expense, a Lear jet and would be there at 7 AM. I heard a sigh of relief as he told me he would have a driver waiting for me at the Marco Island airport. At about 3 AM, I rushed to the office to get my stuff, grabbed a two-liter bottle of diet soda, and ran off to await the arrival of my air ambulance. While I waited, I drank the two-liter bottle of soda.

About 40 minutes into the flight, the two liters of diet soda were ready to make an exit. I then discovered this Lear jet came with just about everything, including a registered nurse named Sandy. The only thing it didn't come with was a bathroom . . . and there was no way I could wait another 90 minutes. There were no bedpans, bottles or containers to help me out. Not to worry. Sandy's got the solution: catheterization. No way! I then asked the pilots what they did on long trips. One of them reached into his leather case, pulled out a plastic sandwich bag with one of those press-and-close tops, emptied out the carrot sticks and handed it to me while giving me a piece of very important advice. "When you seal it, make sure the yellow and blue stripes at the tip turn green."

The plane landed a little before eight. Just before I "de-Leared," the pilot asked me how long I was going to be. The speech was 45 minutes, with a book-signing afterward. I figured I'd be done about noon. "Great," he responded. "We'll wait." How about that? The return trip was free.

The limo got me to the hotel in plenty of time to clean up and prepare. I then gave one of the best presentations of my life. Everything clicked perfectly. Pure adrenaline.

The client was very impressed and appreciative that I was able to honor my commitment and that I was willing to do so, regardless of the cost. Oh yes . . . The cost. It was $7,000. Then to pour a little salt in the wound, they tacked on a 10 percent excise tax, because it was a passenger ticket. Had I let Sandy catheterize me, I would have been a medical passenger and saved $700! And on top of that, there were no frequent flyer miles.

It was an adventure I won't soon forget, especially the bill. But the client was ecstatic, and I've received a lot of spin-off work and great word-of-mouth exposure—not to mention a great personal example to share in my speeches. Keeping the client's needs first always pays. . . . Even when it costs.

Jeff has recouped the $7,000 expense many times over from referrals generated by his enterprising response to solving his problem. He didn't allow himself the luxury of giving up or refusing to pay for his mistake. If basic principles like "always keep your promises to a client" guide your work, you will find unusual solutions to your problems because you will look for them until you do.

Successful salespeople and self-employed professionals not only refuse to run away from adversity, but when it shows up, they use it to their advantage. In 1977, at the age of 22, Hal Becker became the Xerox Corporation's top salesperson in a salesforce of 11,000 people throughout the United States. He didn't get there by selling Xerox machines the way everyone else did. He was always looking for inventive ways to get in the door. In his book *Can I Have 5 Minutes of Your Time?* Hal tells the story of how he landed the best sales of his life during the worst blizzard in Cleveland's history. He bundled himself up and went knocking on office doors, despite the fact that most businesses in the area were closed. All the receptionists and secretaries were at home, so when Hal got an answer, it usually was the boss saying, "Come on in." Because he was able to get right to the decision makers, and they were bored, Hal sold 23 machines in three days—a record that still hasn't been topped.

If you learn not only to cope with adversity but to embrace its potential for unexpected rewards, your business will prosper. Dale Carnegie tells the story of a Florida farmer who was frustrated by his barren land, unable to grow fruit or raise cattle. Because nothing seemed to thrive there but rattlesnakes, he turned his liability into an asset and created one of the world's largest rattlesnake farms. Twenty thousand tourists visit his farm every year. Poison from the fangs of his rattlers is shipped to make antivenom antidotes; rattlesnake skins are sold to make women's shoes and handbags; canned rattlesnake meat is shipped to customers all over the world. Business thrives because the farmer decided to make the best of what he had rather than bemoaning his lousy fate.

 **TRY THIS!**

Identify the rattlesnakes in your front yard. What obstacles, hazards, and handicaps do you presently curse and wish you could get rid of? If removing these snakes isn't working for you, try approaching the problem differently. Is there any way to capitalize on them? Can you turn your version of poisonous snakes into a thriving business opportunity? Are there lemons waiting to become lemonade right in your front yard?

6. ALWAYS KEEP YOUR SENSE OF HUMOR

Laughing at yourself and your circumstances, and laughing with your clients and prospects, is one of the keys to resiliency. Take yourself seriously, but not too seriously, or you will become rigid and breakable when you knock your nose against one of the doors slammed in your face. Find the balance between giving it your all and not letting business burnout eliminate your joy in life. Take it lightly, and be spontaneous. You may even find, as did Martin Rutte, business consultant and coauthor of *Chicken Soup for the Soul at Work,* that keeping a sense of humor actually helps you make the sale. Martin tells this story in his book:

> He was the president of a major advertising firm and I was a very young management consultant. I had been recommended to him by one of his employees who had seen my work and thought I had something to offer. I was nervous. At that stage in my career, it wasn't very often that I got to talk to the president of a company.
>
> The appointment was at 10 AM, for one hour. I arrived early. Promptly at 10, I was ushered into a large and airy room, with furniture upholstered in bright yellow.
>
> He had his shirtsleeves rolled up and a mean look on his face.
>
> "You've only got 20 minutes," he barked.
>
> I sat there, not saying a word.
>
> "I said, you've got only 20 minutes."
>
> Again, not a word.
>
> "Your time's ticking away. Why aren't you saying anything?"
>
> "They're my 20 minutes," I replied. "I can do whatever I want with them."
>
> He burst into laughter.
>
> We then spoke for an hour and a half. I got the job.

Martin's attitude was: "He wants to play? Okay. I'll play." The boss actually was testing him, and by playing the game the way he did, Martin gained respect in his eyes.

Although Martin fervently wanted to make this sale, he didn't lose touch with the fact that on some level, all of sales and business is a game. Play that game with a sense of adventure and fun and a bit of detachment, and you'll not only prosper, but you'll have a much better time, too.

TRY THIS!

Recently, I participated in a dialogue on an Internet discussion list for writers and publishers. The topic was funny rejection stories. Like many professionals, writers and publishers experience more than their fair share of rejection. Those who are successful for the long haul store up amusing rejection stories to entertain themselves and others in lower moments. Perhaps it didn't seem funny at the time, or maybe it did, but laughing at rejection instead of crying about it is one of the best ways to become more resilient.

As part of this discussion, here are two of my favorite sharings from fellow authors:

Andrea Reynolds writes:

> Years ago, I sent a book proposal to a busy literary agent. I included a press release and an order flyer for a creative-date-ideas book I hoped he'd handle called *Let's Do Something Besides Dinner and a Movie,* which I'd already self-published and promoted on national TV with some success. The agent sent a letter rejecting my proposal, saying the book concept would never sell. But also in the envelope was a cheque for $15 from his secretary, who ordered a copy for herself!

Grace Housholder writes:

> My books, *The Funny Things Kids Say Will Brighten Any Day,* are ideal for physician and dentist offices because they have lots of short stories that put people in good moods while they wait for their appointments. One time I took two books to a dermatologist who said he

wanted them for his office. But the next day the receptionist called and said I should come and pick up the
books because the other doctor didn't want them in his
office. (He felt they should have only magazines.) A few
days later when I went to get them the receptionist gave
me a check for the two books. While the books were on
the counter waiting for me a patient saw them and bought
them both! Another time a dentist didn't buy my books
because he said (with a straight face), "No one ever waits
here. We stay on schedule." But his office manager bought
the books for herself. My dentist's receptionist told me that
one patient who had been reading my book came back
the next day to finish reading it!

Andrea and Grace have gone on to be successful published authors, and they will tell you, as will I: The more success you achieve, the more humorous rejection stories you
collect. Adapt to changing circumstances, and you will find
enjoyment in even your rejections. I end this chapter with a
simple suggestion. Think of your worst rejection, the one
that still pains you today. Now, look for the humor in it. It's
there, I assure you!

Keep Your Pipeline Full

WILL AN ATTEMPT TO RETRIEVE THAT ONE COST ME THESE?

A CERTAIN AMOUNT OF DETACHMENT IS CRUCIAL

Devoting yourself passionately to your work while maintaining some level of detachment isn't easy. If you allow your work to define your self-esteem and each piece of good or

119

bad news to drive your emotions, the ups and downs of self-employment will drive you into despair in no time. Therefore, you must learn to separate yourself to some degree from your business without becoming cold and nonchalant. Keeping your pipeline full is one of the best strategies for developing such detachment.

If you have too much riding on one business deal, one sales prospect, or one achievement you desire, invariably you will suffer greater anxiety about the possibility of rejection and failure. Haven't you noticed that when you watch something cook, it seems to take twice as long as when you busy yourself in the kitchen, making good use of the waiting time? "A watched pot never boils" goes the saying. And so it is with waiting for a phone call from a prospect. If you sit in your office waiting for the phone to ring, time moves slowly and your anxiety level increases each day. If you busy yourself in the meantime, you make much better use of your time and you don't have as much chance to worry about being rejected. It's easy to become too attached to your current prospects when you don't have enough solid, qualified leads to pursue.

One key to minimizing your fear of rejection and your response to it is to pursue multiple activities simultaneously so that any specific business disappointment doesn't devastate you.

DIMINISH YOUR DESPERATION

Whenever you focus on scarcity and operate out of desperation, you are less effective. Avoid the vicious cycle so many business owners and salespersons create—low sales, fear of financial ruin, and then poor technique and forceful attempts to make inappropriate sales, which leads to more rejection. When your self-esteem plummets, it becomes much harder to make effective sales calls.

When each potential customer or business contact is few and far between, each possibility takes on enormous significance. If you are an interior decorator and you have four estimates in the works and a handful of warm leads to pursue, you will feel less attached to whether any or all of your estimates turn into paying clients. However, if you submitted only one estimate this month, and you have no other leads to pursue, you will wait anxiously for the phone to ring, and feel crushed if you don't get this particular job—especially if cash-flow is tight, and the electric bill must be paid.

Alex Von Allmen, cofounder of LogoLab, a corporate identity company in Folsom, California, offers this sage advice:

> Prospects sense if you are desperate and they don't want to work with you. Then they reject you more often— they figure something must be wrong with your product or service. It's a vicious cycle. On the other hand, if you have lots of clients and prospects interested in working with you, prospects will beg you to agree to work with *them.*
>
> We spend much more time finding qualified prospects than convincing a prospective customer to buy. We're working with 30 clients right now. Eventually, we'd prefer to work with less clients at one time, but as we grow the business we want to be sure that we're overwhelmed with lots of good, solid leads flowing in.

Ironically, your well-intentioned and self-protective attempts to avoid rejection by making fewer sales calls invites greater rejection overall, because despair will tarnish your ability to present yourself with confidence and self-assurance. It reminds me of my earlier days as a single woman, when I dated for several years before finding my husband, Stephen. When dates were few and far between, each date took on enormous significance, and each disappointing dud was even more heart-wrenching. I'm sure I wasn't as attractive or engaging when I was desperate to find "Mr. Right" either, which lowered my chances of luring the kind of man I was looking for. When I placed an advertisement in the personals and joined a dating service, I was dating several times a month. Then I became much less attached to the results of each date because I knew that there were other "candidates" in the works. My confidence increased, and of course, when I stopped trying so hard to make each date work, my husband, Stephen, showed up on the scene.

DAILY ACTIVITY WILL FILL YOUR PIPELINE

Consistent and constant activity is the key to expanding your prospects and clients. If you wait until you have no clients or customers, then go wild marketing for a few days or weeks when you are frightened and broke, and then retreat back into your shell until the money runs out again, your business is unlikely to prosper. Keeping the pipeline full must be a daily practice, not something you do once or twice a week. When you divide your time between building relationships through networking, responding to client interest, prospecting for new clients, and delivering your services, you will have several projects and prospects in various stages at the same time. *Multitasking is essential for business success!*

Terri Lonier, author of the bestselling book *Working Solo,* shared the following insightful baseball metaphor, which advises "filling up your bases" with plenty of prospects and clients:

We've all experienced the disappointment that comes from that "big" deal going through—quickly followed by the "is that all there is?" feeling. This happens because, as entrepreneurs, our sights are always on the next "big" thing, and we often have moved on to more ambitious goals by the time an achievement is realized. The disappointment also comes, sometimes, because our goals are not realized to the full extent we had anticipated. Instead of a home run, we get a base hit.

Sometimes it pays to get base hits. Pop—you get a runner on first. Pop—you get another base hit and a new runner on first, and the original runner advances to second base. Soon you have a string of base hits and runners on all three bases. Then you come up to the plate and hit a strong drive that goes out of the park, and it's a home run. Because you've been loading up those bases with runners from earlier hits, you score not just one run from the outta-the-park hit, but four.

 **TRY THIS!**

As Terri advises: "Think about your business efforts, and rank them with baseball in mind. Was that achievement a double (and your imaginary runner is now on second base?) Was it almost a home run, but your runner ended up safely at third? Does it pay to attempt a home run and risk an out, or will you select a more conservative strategy and aim for a single?"

This mental exercise keeps your efforts in perspective and makes you realize that even though you have no runs on the scoreboard, you're lining everything up to make it happen. Not every goal you attempt will be, or should be, a home run. Sometimes base hits can be just as valuable to your business in the long term.

What are the home runs and base hits of your business?

For example, one of the home runs of my business is getting a publishing contract. Writing a new column or newsletter, connecting with a media contact, responding to reader mail, and speaking at a convention are all base hits that move me toward my goal of being a bestselling author. When I hit a home run and publish another book, I sell a lot more books because the bases are loaded with contacts, clients, and fans whom I have connected with and assisted in some way during the time between book contracts.

Think about your business in terms of base hits and home runs—it's a fun way to look at your business goals and strategies. List on a sheet of paper or in your journal six home runs you'd like to hit in the next three to six months. Next, identify 10 to 20 base hits—singles, doubles, or triples—that you can make in the next three to six months to load your bases in anticipation of your home runs.   ■■■!

TRY THIS!

Broadening Your Business Revenue— Getting More Base Hits

1. Take a few moments to consider all avenues currently available to you for earning a living and pursuing your business goals. Now list all of the major revenue-producing activities you presently engage in. This can include direct revenue that comes from services delivered and paid for, as well as indirect revenue-producing activities that eventually lead to revenue, such as marketing, attending networking events, and serving on a board of directors.

2. Note the percentage of your time that you currently spend on each of these activities on a weekly or monthly basis. Does your

output of time match your revenue results? If not, do you intentionally spend your time in ways that may not produce revenue but give you other satisfactions? If it's more revenue you want, how must you shift the percentage of time you spend on each activity?

3. List some of the new revenue-producing activities you would like to pursue during the coming year. Think outside the box, and consider new possibilities. What are the next steps you must take to develop these new opportunities?

4. How financially vulnerable are you if any one project or client disappears? How much time do you spend pursuing new customers and opportunities? What can you do in the next three to six months to progress toward this goal?   ...!

THINK LONG TERM

A baseball game lasts only a few hours, so putting a runner on base after the players and the umpires have gone home is useless. In the game of business, however, you can score a base hit today that turns into a home run years from now. Expand your thinking, and undertake activities that may result in rejection today but have the potential for turning into yeses down the road.

For example, as I write this, the crew from T.L. Brossman, a Lancaster, Pennsylvania, company, is sealing our driveway. The owner, Steve Knoff, has been ringing our doorbell for the last three years, trying to sell us his services. Every time he was in the area sealing a neighbor's driveway, he would come by our home and pitch his services: "Because I'm already here doing your neighbor's driveway, would you like us to seal your driveway, too?" Two years in a row, we turned him down—it wasn't in our budget, and we decided to postpone the work one more year. When he rang our bell the third year, it was the right time for us. We called a few neighbors, who gave him glowing references, and we hired him.

We rejected T.L. Brossman's services twice but not because we had anything against him or his company, merely because the timing wasn't right. Steve Knoff has mastered the concept of filling his pipeline. By ringing doorbells every time he does a job in the neighborhood, he willingly takes on plenty of rejection in the hope that someone will say, "Yes—you caught me at the right time."

Schedule your business activity to focus not only on winning short-term sales, but also on developing relationships and staying in touch with long-term prospects. Successful business professionals who are in the right place at the right time often have been in the right place at the wrong time much more often, but they didn't let rejection scare them, and they persisted until the timing was right.

TRY THIS!

Think of five to ten great prospects with whom you would like to do business. These can be people you already know who have turned down your services, or they can be prospects you have yet to meet. Imagine that you *will* do business with them sometime in the next five years, when the timing is right for both of you. Instead of hearing "no, not right now" as "no, not ever," plan how you will stay in touch with these prospects over the next several months and years, if necessary, until the time is right for them to buy.

How can you help them or help the people they care about? How can you mix in the same circles as they do so that your name and business stay familiar to them? How can you stay in touch without being a pest? Consider e-mail newsletters, postcards, quarterly phone calls to check in, or attendance at associations to which they belong to help you increase the odds that they eventually will buy from you. Accept that you may hit a home run with one of these prospects years from now, and don't give up putting runners on the bases until you do. ....!

INCREASE YOUR REFERRALS

Most of us dream of reaching the point in our businesses where clients and prospects beg us to work with them, when we have established such stellar reputations and our services or products are in such demand that we have to turn down business because our schedules are full. That's the best way I know of to reduce the fear of rejection—being in the position to reject prospects rather than the other way around!

Four key actions will increase your referrals:

1. Provide extraordinary value to your current customers so that they can't help but rave about you to all of their friends and neighbors.
2. Ask for referrals.
3. Refer leads to your colleagues, who naturally will want to return the favor.
4. Network, network, network!

These days, delivering average service isn't good enough if you want to build your business by referral. If you merely satisfy a customer, he may not return when he sees a better offer, and he may not speak highly of you to others. Look for ways to wow your customers beyond their expectations. (Chapter 10 provides several creative ideas for delivering superior service.) The best referrals are those you don't even have to ask for, the ones that evolve naturally from happy customers, your best public relations spokespersons.

If you know that your customers are pleased with your product or services, ask them for referrals. You may be too shy to do so, but often customers are eager to share with their networks the benefits you have provided them. They may need only a bit of prompting to come up with warm leads. If your customers feel terrific about what you've given them, they can feel like heroes linking you up with others who need your product or services. Be willing to ask them to think about it.

Put some of your energy into helping your colleagues find the professional help they need, and the good deed will return to you. Pat Weber, a sales consultant, advises that you become a "web weaver":

> Take an active role in putting your prospects together. You hear one say, "I'm really having a difficult time finding a good hairdresser." Offer her the name and telephone number of another customer you have who can fill that need. Or telephone that person while you are with the prospect. Listen to needs your prospects and customers have outside of what you bring to the relationship.

I once asked a holistic practitioner skilled in healing energy work to come to my home for a session when I was a few weeks away from giving birth. While she and I chatted I learned that as a sideline, she performed at elementary schools and daycare centers as a fairy godmother. She has a closetful of costumes, and she performs various skits, depending on the age group. In the middle of the discussion, I said, "Excuse me, I've got a phone call to make." I immediately called the daycare center where my two daughters spend their days and raved to the center director about this woman's unique talents. The director asked for one of her brochures, and the connection was made. Notice that I didn't wait until later, when and if I got around to it, and it took me all of three minutes. The practitioner appreciated me making the effort, whether or not my contact hired her. As I meet people, I always flip through my mental rolodex to see how the people I know could benefit each other. The previous name of my company was The Critical Link because I enjoy making these connections so much.

Be of service to your colleagues and community, and watch how fast your pipeline fills.

"Networking—Nuisance or Necessity?" is the name of a seminar that my friend and colleague, Deb Haggerty, offers to help professionals build their businesses through referrals. Deb reminds us of the secret to effective networking:

> Networking is about giving as well as getting. It is mutual sharing of information and business leads. You must be willing to share your information and contacts with others, as well as leads for them, if you ever hope to gain from the experience. Successful networking means giving as much as or more than you take.

Over the last 20 years, I have seen the look and feel of networking change a great deal. Years ago, networking meant reluctantly going to local chamber of commerce and business association meetings and awkwardly trying to get your business card into the hands of as many attendees as possible. These events reminded us introverted types of high school days, when we went to school dances and feared being stuck on the sidelines as wallflowers. Networking was so uncomfortable we'd find excuses not to attend business events, or when we did go, we'd stick like glue to the colleagues with whom we already were acquainted.

The key to making networking events more enjoyable is to let go of the events as a means to a sale and, instead, to focus on getting to know other professionals in your community. Nancy Roebke, executive director of ProfNet, a networking organization designed to help professionals find more business, reminds us: "The chances of actually making a sale at these events is slim. People haven't had a chance to get to know, like, and trust you yet."

Bob Burg, a sales expert and author of *Endless Referrals,* shares some great tips for making a positive connection when conversing at a networking event:

> Let's pretend someone just asked what you do for a living. When you answer, it just happens to be something that person really needs.
>
> For instance, imagine that you are a stockbroker. You responded not by saying, "I'm a stockbroker," or even "I'm a financial planner," but instead by giving a short statement, such as "I help people create and manage wealth."
>
> The person looks at you and says, "What a coincidence. My spouse and I were just talking about the fact that we are very weak in that area and need to do something about it. We're working hard, but we have nothing put away for the later years. We know we definitely need to talk to a person such as yourself right away."
>
> Let's face it. At this point, everything inside you wants to go Yesss!!!!
>
> That, unfortunately, would not be the correct response. As tempting as it might be to try to set up an appointment with that person and his spouse right on the spot, realize that they are just not ready yet. The "know you, like you, trust you" stage has not yet been established. Bombarding that person right now will do just the opposite of what you want to accomplish. Instead, go right back to asking questions about him and his business, which are

open ended. Ask questions that will make him or her feel good about being in a conversation with you, even though you've just met and he or she hardly knows you.

I have ten questions in my personal arsenal. You'll notice that they are all friendly and fun to answer and will tell you something about the way that person thinks. You'll never need or have the time to ask all ten questions during any one conversation. Still, you should internalize them. Know them well enough that you are able to ask the ones you deem appropriate for the particular conversation and time frame.

Here are the ten questions:

1. How did you get your start in the widget business?
2. What do you enjoy most about your profession?
3. What separates you and your company from the competition?
4. What advice would you give someone starting in the widget business?
5. What one thing would you do with your business if you knew you could not fail?
6. What significant changes have you seen take place in your profession through the years?
7. What do you see as coming trends in the widget business?
8. Describe the strangest or funniest incident you've experience in your business.
9. What ways have you found to be the most effective for promoting your business?
10. What one sentence would you like people to use in describing the way you do business?

And the question that Bob says gets the best response . . .

11. How can I know whether someone I am talking to would be a good prospect for you?

 **TRY THIS!**
■ ■ ■

Don't use Bob's questions in a conversation with a colleague at a networking event unless you are willing to answer these same questions yourself. Therefore, take a moment to reflect on each of the questions about your own business.

Although I attend networking and association events in person, I do most of my networking through the Internet, by actively participating in several mailing lists and discussion groups, offering my expertise to dozens of Web sites and linking up professionals from all over the world. Networking in person in your local community may still be essential, depending on your business, but don't limit yourself to that. The Internet has opened up new and enjoyable ways to actively network with professionals from around the globe. If you haven't yet gotten yourself an e-mail address and the ability to surf the Web through a Web browser, do it now! It will be an excellent investment of your time and resources.   ...!

A final thought on networking: As we discussed in Chapter 3, accept your limits, identify the kinds of networking you'd find enjoyable and helpful to your business, and don't worry if you can't do it all. You may never join Rotary or an Internet discussion group. You may do your best networking when you volunteer at your church or help run the local Boy Scouts. Some form of connecting with and serving professionals in a network who can refer other professionals to you is essential to your success. You choose the form you are most comfortable with and therefore likely to commit to on a regular basis.

HELPFUL TIPS FOR BUILDING RAPPORT WITH A PROSPECT

Besides offering a valued product or service and networking to expand your referral base, filling your pipeline also must involve selling your business effectively to strangers or warm leads. I have warned of the danger of believing that if you say the right words or act the right way, every person will want to be your customer. Some rejection in the sales process is inevitable; you must accept that. That said, sales techniques designed to help you develop better rapport with prospective clients certainly will improve your ability to keep your pipeline full by alluring more interested prospects.

Hundreds of books are available that teach a variety of sales techniques. You will find several in this book's bibliography and recommended resources section. I encourage you to invest in some sales training resources to help you develop your sales presentation skills.

Grover Gouker, a professional speaker and sales trainer from Lancaster, Pennsylvania, introduced me to his technique for responding to objections when presenting your product or services. If you can't do it naturally, the sales technique may come across as forced. But if you can integrate the empathic attitude behind the technique, and your compassion is genuine, this approach offers a successful and more enjoyable way to sell. Grover says:

> Most salespeople view objections as something to defend against. A prospect says, "The price is too high," and the salesperson responds argumentatively, "What do you mean, the price is too high?" What good does that statement do? You can *react* with something that sounds like you are saying to the prospect, "You're an idiot," or you can *respond* with a statement that communicates,

"You probably have a good reason you feel that way. I respect you."

I teach salespeople to respond with a positive statement of understanding immediately following an objection. I call these PSUs. PSUs are empathic rather than defensive. They communicate that I'm on the prospect's side. I've got his best interests at heart. Here's an example:

Prospect: "I've been doing business with another company for 15 years, and I don't want to switch."

Traditional salesperson: "Maybe it's about time to change. They've been taking you for a ride."

Respond with this PSU instead: "I appreciate that kind of loyalty."

Here is another example:

Prospect: "The price of your sales course is too high."

Traditional salesperson: "You'll appreciate the value after I explain to you everything you will be getting for this price."

Respond with this PSU instead: "If I were in your position, I would be concerned about any investment I'm going to make." Or "I know what you mean. Rarely do we have $495 sitting around that isn't already spoken for."

Then, after the PSU, I make sure I'm dealing with only one objection. I'd say something like:

"If we could meet that particular problem and solve it for you, is there anything else that would keep you from taking this sales course?"

If the prospect says, "No, the only problem is that it costs too much," I can show her how the $495 spent on the course will be returned immediately in increased income, or I can negotiate a payment arrangement that would suit her needs.

Gretchen Plemmons, cofounder of Cyber-Pet, from Libby, Montana, spends a great deal of her time on the telephone prospecting advertisers for her 800-page Web site that includes a dog and cat magazine, a rescue database, breed information, chat rooms, a breeder showcase, and a wealth of information for pet owners. Gretchen puts a mirror on her desk and smiles at it while she makes her telephone calls. She insists, "At first, you'll be self-conscious about it, but after awhile, it will make a huge difference. It will change your tone of voice."

Pat Weber, author of *Sales Skills for an Unfair Advantage,* shares this simple tip for one of the most important tools for establishing rapport—remembering someone's name:

> It's as easy as 1-2-3 by (1) using their name immediately when you are introduced: "It's great to meet you here, Betty Tracy; (2) then during the conversation when you ask a question of them, ask the question using their name: "How long have you been a member of this organization, Betty?"; and (3) the third time is a charm for your memory when you use their name either when someone else joins your conversation or one of you leaves to mingle with another small group. Use a person's name three times when you first meet and your memory will make it an easy task for you.

I was intrigued to learn that rapport building can be affected by something as simple as a handshake. In July 1998, *Entrepreneur* magazine reported a significant study, conducted by Dr. Allen Konopacki of the Incomm Center for Trade Show Research in Chicago. The study suggests that the handshake is far more than a simple gesture—it's the beginning of a relationship. With the help of a group of students, Dr. Konopacki conducted an experiment in which a quarter was left in the coin return of a public telephone. If a stranger took the coin after using the phone, a student walked up and asked whether the person had seen the quarter. The result? Sixty percent of the 75 people asked lied to the students and said they had not seen the quarter. In the next series of 75 confrontations, the students introduced themselves with a handshake before asking about the quarter. Surprisingly, less than 15 percent of the strangers lied to the students. The study concluded that handshakes improved the quality of the interactions, producing, as Dr. Konopacki says, "a higher degree of intimacy and trust within a matter of seconds."

The "handshake effect," as Dr. Konopacki refers to it, also applies to salespeople. "If a person walks into a store or an exposition and is greeted with a handshake," he says, "he or she is more likely to remember the exhibit and spend more time with the salesperson, who ends up getting a better quality contact or lead."

Essential to developing rapport is to be genuine in your actions. You can tell when a sales professional tries to manipulate you by using one of the latest sales techniques for establishing rapport. One of my pet peeves is when sales professionals try the oldest trick in the book: "Is next Monday or Thursday better for you?" (when I haven't even indicated interest in meeting with them to check out what they have to offer). When I feel like I am talking to a scripted parrot or a computer, not a real human being, and when I feel as if any objection I make will be met with a well-rehearsed comeback, I can't get off the phone fast enough. Sales techniques are most effective when the customer doesn't have a clue that you are using them! The suggestions in this chapter work best when they become natural to you—extensions of how you do business rather than manipulation techniques you try to master.

GIVE AWAY YOUR SKILLS AND EXPERTISE

Without question, one of the greatest secrets to my professional success and my full pipeline is that I give away my expertise to thousands of people. I write and produce three free online newsletters for small-business professionals, which go to more than 30,000 entrepreneurs all over the world. I've given my syndicated column, "Advice from A–Z," to many small publications and Web sites that have no budgets to pay me. I spend hours a month giving my expertise to media professionals, Web sites, networking colleagues, and readers who write me with questions after reading my books.

Each of you must decide how much of your time you will give away without direct compensation. I enjoy the spirit of giving, but I'm not entirely altruistic. Giving away my expertise is an effective tool for establishing my authority, developing an international network, and keeping my name in people's minds. You never know when it will pay off for you, which is part of the fun. For example, one of my columns appeared in a small newspaper in Oregon. Turns out, unbeknownst to me, the Work and Family columnist for *The Wall Street Journal* happens to live in the town where the column appeared. She read my column and loved it, and after contacting me, she recommended my first book, *Honey, I Want to Start My Own Business,* in her column as one of the best work and family books in 1996. You can't pay for a *Wall Street Journal* recommendation like that. Giving of myself as much as possible always comes back to me many times over.

TRY THIS!

For a moment, let go of your concerns about how to make money, sell more product, expand your client base, and so on. Shift your thinking to this question:

Who am I in the position to help today?

Ask yourself the question every day, and look for opportunities to be of service. Your business surely will profit.

KEEPING YOURSELF MOTIVATED AND ON TRACK

I mentioned earlier that the secret to bringing in the business you need is consistent daily marketing activity and sales. Most of you would much rather deliver your services than market or sell them or you wouldn't have bought this book. Find some marketing activities that are painless for you—service that you genuinely enjoy—so that it doesn't always feel like hard work. For example, I really enjoy writing the newsletters that I put out six times a month as one of my marketing tools.

If you procrastinate or make excuses for not doing enough marketing or sales activity, find yourself a professional buddy to whom you can be accountable.

Miriam Otte, a small-business consultant and author of *Marketing with Speeches and Seminars: Your Key to More Clients and Referrals,* set up a daily system with a colleague that keeps her on track toward her goals:

> My dear friend, Pam (who lives hundreds of miles away), and I made a pact. At the end of each work day,

" I HAVE A TON OF CALLS I SHOULD BE MAKING TODAY. "

we report what five marketing activities we did that day. Talk about built-in accountability! It really works, and it doesn't take much extra effort.

If it's 3:00 PM and I've got only one thing on "Pam's list," I know it's time to start hustling. Some days, we do many more than five. Other times, it's a challenge to accomplish one. The encouragement and support is always there, though, and although our niche markets are quite different, we get ideas from one another.

If you are active online, setting up such a relationship with an online marketing buddy will help you benefit from daily, inexpensive accountability. If you aren't an e-mail afi-cionado, try to find a colleague in your community with whom you can meet once a week over coffee or lunch or check in by telephone every day. You'll find that your marketing efforts increase dramatically.

INCREASING THE AMOUNT OF REJECTION MAKES IT LESS PAINFUL

I'll remind you of the statement I made at the beginning of this chapter: *One key to minimizing your fear of rejection and your response to it is to pursue multiple activities simulta-neously so that any specific business disappointment doesn't devastate you.*

To pursue several activities simultaneously so that you minimize your fear of rejection, you actually increase the fre-quency of rejection because you actively present yourself to more people who can reject you!

When you widen the span of your business activity, you may be rejected more often, but you don't dwell on each re-jection as much because you have many runners on base. It stings when you lose an opportunity you hoped for, but you don't have time to mope around for long. When your pipeline is full of possibilities, you never lose hope.

Focus Your Efforts

TRADITIONAL SALES TECHNIQUES
ARE MISLEADING

For years, the traditional sales model taught that if you spoke the right words in your presentation, practiced a response to every conceivable objection, and perfected a powerful close, you would get the sale—no matter whom the prospect.

Becoming rejection-proof demands a paradigm shift: Instead of trying to make each sale and worrying about rejection, *you* become the rejector! When you decide whom you want to sell to and service, and you reject unqualified prospects, you'll become more confident and take control of your business.

This attitude is much easier to adopt when your pipeline is full and you aren't desperate for clients, which is why this chapter follows the last—"Keep Your Pipeline Full." When you are broke and scared, panic won't lead to more sales, only more rejection because you will spend too much time pursuing inappropriate customers.

THREE-FOOT RULE

During the two years I sold a multilevel marketed product, I learned about the "three-foot rule." In short, the three-foot rule means that anyone standing within three feet of you is a prospect until proven otherwise. I was encouraged by my upline and successful people in the industry to see everyone in the whole world as my prospect. Hats off to those MLMers and other sales professionals who can use the three-foot rule effectively. For me, it was disastrous, and I ultimately left the business because I didn't like the obsession it created.

I was selling an herbal supplement that had provided me with outstanding health benefits, and anyone in the world could benefit from using it. But when, in my mind, the whole world became my prospect, I stopped enjoying the business and my personal relationships. I couldn't relax and chat with a friend, neighbor, family member, or stranger without looking for a way to bring my product or business opportunity into the conversation. If someone I knew and cared about was ill, even if she was entirely closed to using my product,

I became obsessed with finding a way to convince her to try it. I was so drawn to manipulate every personal encounter into a sale that I didn't take time off from selling when I needed to. I stopped appreciating relationships for what they were.

I don't like seeing my world as one of constant prospects. It makes me feel sleazy and desperate, and I don't hear half of what anyone says to me because too often my focus is on finding a way to introduce my business into the discussion.

Incorporate the spirit of the three-foot rule into your life if it helps you detach from each prospect, knowing that if this one doesn't buy, thousands will. Remember the rule when you need to be reminded that prospects may show up in the most unlikely places if you keep your mind open and engage the world with a positive attitude and a true love for your product or services. But don't turn the entire universe into a gigantic rolodex for your business. It will make you a boring and obnoxious person.

Jay Leno, in his autobiography, *Leading with My Chin*, tells an absurd, true story of what happened to him when a salesperson allowed the three-foot rule to get out of control.

Early in Jay's budding career as a comedian, when money was definitely an issue for him, Jay was mugged and the thieves stole $70 from him. When he stopped at the police station to file a report, the officer took down all the information, then said, "I'll have your 70 bucks back for you tonight." To Jay's shock and dismay, the crafty policeman arrived at his door at midnight that night, wearing off-duty clothing and carrying a small suitcase. The police officer opened the suitcase on the table and told Jay that he would help him get his money back—by selling Echo Silverware! Turns out, the policeman was a moonlighting salesman, and he must have viewed every victim as a potential prospect.

Here is the three-foot rule taken too far. Perhaps the officer was able to make a sale every now and again with this outrageous approach, but he'd be rejected most of the time because he was not selling to qualified prospects. He also wasn't the kind of person that most of us would respect or want to emulate (though you do have to admire his chutzpah!).

THE JAFFE 3–5 RULE

I've developed my own strategy for business success that I call the Jaffe 3–5 rule. Its purpose is the opposite of the three-foot rule: the 3–5 rule helps you *narrow* your focus, target your market, and be more successful as a result. In doing so, you experience less rejection because you approach those customers and prospects most likely to buy from you, and you make the best use of your time.

The 3–5 rule goes like this: To prosper in your business, focus your efforts on no more than three to five major target markets, using no more than three to five primary marketing tools, and making the most of your three to five greatest business skills. Be sure you spend your time in three to five major business responsibilities, and if possible delegate the rest.

As a successful business professional, you probably use the 3–5 rule without even knowing it.

3–5 business skills. Even if your business forces you to broaden your duties, you probably are exceptionally good at three to five major responsibilities. You will learn to do one or two more responsibilities if you have to, but they are not your natural gift. You should delegate the rest of your daily tasks to a business partner, employees, or other contracted help.

3–5 business activities. You spend 80 percent of your time doing three major business activities and 20 percent doing one or two minor business activities that spin off from the first three. If this isn't the case for you, you probably spread yourself too thin to be effective.

3–5 target markets. Eighty percent of your revenue comes from one to three major business markets, and 20 percent comes from smaller markets outside of your major three. (Take a look at your current revenue stream; does this hold true for you?)

3–5 sales and marketing approaches. Though you may vary your marketing and sales activities, your comfort zone, type of business, and skill level lead you to select three to five primary ways to market and sell your services or product to prospective buyers. Because you tend to use the same sales approach repetitively, you lose some of your fear of rejection as you build proficiency in whatever method you choose. Though you consider experimenting with new approaches from time to time, you are unlikely to depart too often from what generally works for you.

Take a look at the chart in Figure 7.1, which shows how the 3–5 rule works for three very different types of businesses. Kathy Whittington is an independent area manager for Arbonne International, a network marketing health and wellness company. She distributes herbal and botanical-based personal care products person to person and through her downline. Gretchen Plemmons is cofounder, with her husband, of Cyber-Pet, an Internet resource for dog and cat enthusiasts, offering an encyclopedic library of articles for owners and breeders, rescue and breed clubs, product advertising, breed information, chats, and posting boards. The chart compares these businesses to mine—writing and consultant work.

You should notice two things:

1. The three of us engage in entirely different professional activities because our businesses are very dissimilar.

2. However, because the 3–5 rule works for all three of us, you will see a great deal of consistency within each business, with the same key phrases and activities cropping up over and over again. That is the way it should be. The secret to success is to find what works, focus on your ideal market, and then keep doing it again and again.

FIGURE 7.1: *THE JAFFE 3–5 RULE*
■ ■ ■

	Business Skills	Responsibilities
Azriela Jaffe, Anchored Dreams, consultancy	Writing Professional speaking Coaching	1. Write books, newsletters, and columns 2. Give speeches at conventions 3. Participate in media interviews and Internet discussion groups 4. Coach clients 5. Bookkeeping
Kathy Whittington, Arbonne International, network marketing health and beauty products	Coaching Personal selling Administrative details	1. Train new distributors 2. Present product/business to prospective customers 3. Sell product to current customers 4. Package and mail product 5. Bookkeeping
Gretchen Plemmons, Cyber-Pet, Internet-based resource and retail	Phone sales Bringing in advertisers Maintaining site content	1. Telephone sales to prospective advertisers 2. Put together advertising deals 3. Gather articles that improve Web content 4. Administrative details for mail-order business

	Target Market	Primary Marketing Activities
Azriela Jaffe, Anchored Dreams, consultancy	Self-employed professionals Spouses of self-employed professionals Professionals who serve and teach self-employed professionals Professionals who aspire to be self-employed	Books, newsletters, columns Media expert—TV, radio, print appearances Speaking and delivering workshops/keynotes Participating in Internet discussion groups
Kathy Whittington, Arbonne International, network marketing health and beauty products	Health conscious consumers Beauty conscious professional women Moms who desire to work at home Men who desire health and beauty Individuals seeking weight loss	Networking at meetings and associations Referrals from current customers Donating gift certificates Cold calling on bridal salons, doctors' offices
Gretchen Plemmons, Cyber-Pet, Internet-based resource and mail-order catalog	Potential advertisers for site Dog and cat breeders Current dog and cat owners Prospective dog and cat owners	Follow-up calls to application on Web site Mailings to prospective advertisers Expanding and improving Web content

SAY NO!

To use the 3–5 rule, you must be willing to say no, to turn away business if it will distract your attention from where your focus belongs—on your three to five major business activities. If you say yes to every customer who wants your services just because he is willing to pay you something, you can become too distracted and short on time to focus your energy on your most lucrative and high-potential markets. Stick to a business plan that directs your focus to your primary markets.

Alex and Tania Von Allmen are cofounders of LogoLab, a California corporate identity company that helps emerging companies figure out who they are and how to communicate that image to their marketplaces. Alex shared the following anecdote to illustrate the power of saying no:

> Have you ever heard about the way they catch monkeys in Africa? They drill a hole in a pumpkin and then put some bait inside of it. The hole in the pumpkin is just large enough so that the monkey can put its hand in, but when it grasps the bait, the monkey can't pull its fist out. Because the monkey never will let go of the food, the hunters have an easy target. They come around and shoot the monkeys.
>
> Business owners who don't have enough prospects become like those monkeys—hanging on when it's time to let go.

Being successful in business is not just about making the sale. You also must learn when it's time to let go of a prospect, a job, or a particular market segment that doesn't really need your services or product or won't pay for it.

"LET'S LET THEM GO, AND MOVE ALONG, STANLEY. THEY'RE JUST NOT INTERESTED IN OUR PRODUCTS."

Letting go of a disinterested prospect takes courage but inevitably results in more and easier sales, as your energy and time become available for more suitable prospects that appear.

 **TRY THIS!**

See how your current business measures up to the 3–5 rule.

Business skills. Consider the top three to five business skills you bring to your business. Do you spend time doing anything that you lack the skill to do well? If so, how can you delegate this responsibility? If you don't have the cash to pay anyone, consider bartering your services.

Business activities. Which three to five major business activities compose the majority of your week? If this list includes more than three to five major activities, that might explain any fatigue, burnout, or lack of profitability you experience.

Target market. Define three to five target markets for your product or services.

Sales and marketing tools. Identify three to five primary means you use, or wish to use, to market and sell your business.

■■■!

SEVEN TECHNIQUES FOR FOCUSING YOUR EFFORTS AND MINIMIZING REJECTION

1. Identify What You Are Not and Will Not Try to Be

To figure out who you are and how you want to be known in the marketplace, a good first step is to get clear about what you are *not* and don't want to pretend to be.

Dave Markham is co-owner with his wife, Sue, of the Idaho firm Venture Outdoors, a travel adventure company that exposes people to wilderness areas while providing the most comfort possible. After being in the travel business for 15 years, Dave recognizes the customers he's *not* designed to serve:

A large portion of the people calling us don't care about the customized service we offer. It's like the difference between buying something at Wal-mart versus a specialty store. Some people are willing to go to a specialty store to get better service, even if it costs more. We're not a big company with a big name, with hundreds of trips all over the world. We offer a specialized service to those people who are looking for the unique benefits of the trips we offer.

A large number of customers who call inquiring about his trips reject Dave's travel services, but he has learned not to take those rejections personally. His focus is on how to reach and serve those customers who already want what he has to offer.

Kay Rice is co-owner of Brush Ranch Camp, a Santa Fe, New Mexico, children's summer camp that has been operating since 1956. The camp specializes in the arts, adventure-based programs, and sports. Families come back year after year. Kay can predict when a caller won't buy in just a minute or two:

> Plenty of camps have a lot of glitz and glitter—they helicopter in a celebrity to begin their color war, paying thousands of dollars for the celebrity to start it off. We have a boringly predictable program that works really well. Families know they will be treated with respect and problems will be cared for and not swept under the carpet. When the first question someone asks about our camp is the price, I know this won't be a child for us. If cost is the primary issue instead of the benefits we offer, [the customer] won't come to our camp even if she could come up with the money.

Kay takes a few moments with such callers to refer them to alternative camps that might be what they are looking for. She doesn't sweat it when she doesn't make the sale. Kay is confident in what she has to offer, and she understands that her camp will not be a match for every interested child and parent. If she tried to compete with bigger, more glamorous camps, it would distract her from what Brush Ranch Camp has been doing so well for more than 40 years. Spending too much time trying to convince first-time callers with financial concerns that her camp experience is worth the money she charges would deplete her energy. Brush Ranch Camp sticks with what Kay knows it does well, and the payoff is a successful camp with a huge referral business.

 **TRY THIS!**

Write down on a piece of paper or in your journal five to ten statements of what your company is not and will not try to be.

■■■!

2. Identify What You Are and What You Wish to Be Known For

A natural evolution from the step above—clarifying what you are not—is to understand what you *are*, as well as the professional reputation you wish to develop. This may be in the form of a mission or benefit statement that you've already spelled out. For example, my mission statement, which appears on my stationery is: "Anchored Dreams provides practical assistance and emotional support to individuals, couples, and partners in business."

If you are a CPA, it would be more powerful to explain, "I'm a CPA specializing in helping family-owned businesses become more profitable," than to say simply, "I'm a CPA," when someone asks, "What do you do?" Integrating your specialty and target market into one sentence helps people understand the kinds of referrals you'd most appreciate when you converse at a networking event.

Let's say you are an architect specializing in custom-made houses costing $500,000 or more. You would waste your time and experience plenty of rejection if you tried to sell your services to customers looking for homes in the $200,000 to $300,000 price range. Those customers are unlikely to be able to afford your fees or to take advantage of your unique expertise. Therefore, your mission statement might be something like: "I specialize in designing homes that provide the wealthy with the special features and amenities that are important to them. Not one of my houses will ever be exactly the same as another. I wish to be known as *the* premier architect for the wealthy in the Boston area and vicinity." And if someone were to ask you in a networking event, "What do you do?" you could say, "I design custom homes for the wealthy in the Boston area."

 **TRY THIS!**
■ ■ ■

Create a mission statement in one to three sentences that expresses the special benefits and features you provide your market.   ■ ■ ■ ▪

3. Distinguish Three to Five Target Markets That Match Your Statements for #1 and #2

Now that you have defined what you want to be known for in your industry, get clear about who you want to serve. Identify three to five major markets for your services or product—groups of potential customers who share common characteristics and need what you have to offer. At this stage, don't worry about getting too specific; just identify the larger segments of your market. Some examples follow.

A landscaper specializes in caring for lawns, trimming shrubs, and designing flower beds. Her target market is homeowners and residential communities within a 15-mile radius. The customers most likely to purchase her services are dual-career couples who have no time for lawn care and senior citizens who can't handle the manual labor anymore.

A self-employed psychologist offers a broad range of counseling but hopes to build his practice from referrals in three markets: (1) employers referring troubled employees for short-term counseling the employers pay for, (2) members of his church community who seek family counseling, and (3) couples considering divorce—his specialty from graduate school.

Though the landscaper and the psychologist will serve customers who don't fall into their targeted markets, they should focus most of their time on penetrating their markets of choice. Knowing who composes your target market makes it much easier to design a marketing approach that will accomplish your desired results.

For example, if the landscaper knows that senior citizens are a target market, she may offer a free workshop to a senior citizen group in the community about easy lawn care that doesn't take too much time or money. The workshop's purpose would be to show senior citizens how they can do much of the work themselves, but if she impresses the group with her knowledge and empathy for their concerns, the landscaper probably would pick up a couple of clients who need more work than they can manage themselves, as well as referrals.

The psychologist who specializes in employer assistance programs might create a stress management seminar for managers and supervisors to demonstrate to company management his counseling skills and explain how employees could benefit from his training and experience.

 **TRY THIS!**
■ ■ ■

To select your three to five target markets, consider the following questions:

1. What unique expertise do you offer that would benefit particular markets?
2. With whom do you naturally establish rapport?
3. Which markets mesh with your preferred sales approach and your desire to avoid certain kinds of rejection?
4. Who needs what you offer?
5. Who has the means and is willing to pay for what you offer?
6. What markets are easily accessible to you?
7. With whom do you enjoy spending time?
8. What kinds of customers have been the most profitable for you in the past?
9. What kinds of customers offer you qualified and profitable referrals?
10. Who can you serve better than your competitors?　　■■■!

4. Pare Down

Think about those activities that you do on a daily or weekly basis out of habit, activities that do not serve your business as well as other projects could. For example, do you procrastinate on sales calls by spending hours surfing Web sites? Does your Internet activity bring you business, or do you hide behind the Net because you don't risk rejection when you surf? Do you regularly attend a business lunch that never has brought you business but costs $14 every time you eat? Have any of the magazines or publications you read become extraneous to your business or too costly to be a good use of your time?

You don't have to completely eliminate an activity or affiliation if you decide to pare down for the time being. As a personal example, I am a member of the National Speakers Association, which has phenomenal annual conventions. In 1998, the convention came to Philadelphia (only a few hours from my home), and I planned to attend.

After much thought, however, using the wisdom I share with you in this section of the book, I decided to stay home. I know I would have had a fabulous time. I would have made some new connections, and it could have helped my business. But the convention was held during a time when my speaking was back-burnered because I had just given birth to our son, Elijah. My primary focus was on my writing (including this book), and although I knew I'd be doing plenty of professional speaking in the future, it wasn't a good use of three days and several hundred dollars. Tempting though the convention was, I spent those three days hunkered down in front of my computer, fulfilling my writing obligations.

Hilton Johnson, a sales coach and lifelong salesperson, uses the following technique when he wants to either close a sale or take an indecisive prospect off of his list if that person has taken up a lot of his time:

> The next time your prospect hesitates to move forward with your proposal or keeps giving you resistance/objections, say this to him: "Based on what you're saying, this is probably not for you. Shall I close your file?"
>
> Selling is a game, and fear of loss is a great motivator. When you stop the game, many people fear that they will lose out on something important, and therefore they will show more interest in your proposal.
>
> This little "take-away" works best with prospects who are stalling because it conveys that you're not desperate for the sale.

 **TRY THIS!**
■ ■ ■

Take action this week to end or reduce one or two business activities that distract you from your main focus and are not profitable or synergistic to your primary goals.

List the tasks and responsibilities that consume your time during a typical week. Note those customers whom you have been pursuing for potential sales. Scan these lists with the following questions in mind:

1. Are any prospects unlikely to ever become customers? Is it time to let them go? (Differentiate between unlikely prospects and prospects who simply need multiple communications and a longer time before they buy.)
2. Do certain business activities take up a lot of time and distract you from your focus rather than support it?
3. Do you do anything that you could keep in the marketing mix but do less of if it isn't one of your three to five major activities and it takes too much time?
4. Are specific customers or groups of customers more trouble than they are worth, costing more in time and energy than they typically bring you in business or referrals? Who are you unlikely to ever make happy? (Note: You may keep working with a particular customer, even if she is challenging, or unprofitable, because she is a regular source of referrals.)　　■ ■ ■ ￼

5. Create Exclusivity

When you make your product or services more exclusive, you add value to them. When customers feel as though they are part of a special group, they will pay more for the privilege of belonging, especially if what accompanies the "membership" is superlative customer service and products targeted precisely to what the customers need. Is a Mercedes Benz worth $50,000 or more? It is to the people who buy or lease one. They are willing to pay for the privilege of both owning a car that handles beautifully and receiving extraordinary customer care. Customers who purchase an item that most of the world cannot afford are proud of their accomplishments. If Mercedes priced its vehicles too low, the company would lose a portion of its upper-class buyers, who no longer would view owning a Mercedes as a status symbol.

 **TRY THIS!**

Look at your business and all of the products and services you provide. Can you create a feeling of exclusivity in some part of your business? Consider the following possibilities:

1. Raise prices for a target market in exchange for more value-added benefits.
2. Establish a minimum standard customers must meet to be eligible for your services.
3. Offer a discount on one of your products for subscribers or members of a special group or subscriber list.
4. Limit the time when customers can take advantage of a special offer, after which the price will increase.
5. Communicate that you have a limited amount of a particular product and will sell it only until you have emptied inventory.
6. Create a subgroup of clients who pay a membership fee to belong to a special group, which receives additional benefits.

6. Create Niches within Your Niches

A few years ago, I watched with great interest the television profile of a dry-cleaning business that is thriving not because it is the best dry-cleaner on the block, but because it came up with a unique marketing idea to get customers through the door. The dry-cleaner's general market was anyone living within a certain radius who needed dry-cleaning services. The business could, like most dry-cleaners, compete on price and service, but it identified a niche it wanted to capture—serving the single professionals in the area.

The husband and wife who ran this dry-cleaning establishment started putting pictures of eligible singles on their lobby wall, creating the area's largest personals ad. Word spread quickly throughout the singles community, and pictures of eligible and looking-to-date singles soon crammed every available space in the lobby. When a single professional dropped off his or her clothing to be cleaned, the owners offered to take a polaroid picture and hang it on the wall with a phone number. Before you know it, most of the single professionals in the area were bringing their clothes to this establishment to be cleaned—just to check out the wall!

It is not enough to identify your three to five biggest markets, as I asked you to do in section number 3. Although that action alone surely will reduce your rejection experience, to really focus your energies in the most profitable way, subdivide those markets further into specialty areas.

For example, Paul Swengler owns TexTperts, a Hawaiian company that provides electronic publishing alternatives to paper. Paul tells the following story from his earlier days as a Prentice Hall book representative, selling law books door to door. His target market at the time was attorneys, but he spotted a niche within the larger market:

I cold-called an attorney one day. I entered the office, and I see a guy on his hands and knees with a yardstick in his hand. He looked up, and I said, "Hi. I'm looking for Steve."

He responded, "Who wants to know?" as he stood up. I assumed he was Steve. "I'm Paul," I said. "I just took over as the Prentice Hall rep in this area. I wanted to meet the attorneys in my territory."

With great force, he said, "I DON'T BUY BOOKS!"

"Well, Steve, you are an attorney, and it would be malpractice to dispense law without research. What do you do for reference?"

"I go to the law library. It's just a block away."

We were still standing in the reception area. "Great! You know that the law library is the largest buyer of my books. If you have a minute, I'd like to tell you what it just bought. See, if you and others use my books, it will likely buy more. What areas do you practice in?"

As he answers me, we started heading into his office. Guess what? There were books on his bookshelf.

After about two or three minutes, he reveals he does domestic law. I said, "Gee, Steve, the only thing I have in that area is a desktop reference, a Boy Scout handbook with cookbook forms in the back. The law library didn't buy this one because it's a practice manual and [the library] likes treatises. I don't know—is it something that would fit on your desk?"

Bingo. $135 and about ten minutes later, I left. The key is listening.

I called on him about eight months later. He had moved, and this time I was standing in front of the receptionist, who was positioned immediately to the right of his door. I walked up to her and loud enough for Steve to hear, I said, "Hi. I'm Paul from Prentice Hall. I know

Steve doesn't buy books. I just wanted to make a courtesy call on him. Is he in?"

We met, and he purchased another $150 worth of books. He was always happy with what he purchased from me but never understood how I could take a rejection and turn it into a sale.

It's not that Steve didn't buy books. It was that he didn't buy libraries. He wanted the equivalent of a hand saw, not a chain saw. He would easily spend $200 but not $2,000. I knew that right away when I saw what was on his shelf.

Martha Rogers and Don Peppers, cofounders of the consulting firm, Marketing 1to1, are two of the leading authorities in the world on what they refer to as "mass customization"—that is, reaching large groups of customers in a personalized way to enhance sales and service. Even the largest multibillion dollar organizations can use the latest in technological wizardry to identify, reach, then serve their customers with superlative customer service.

Martha tells the story of how the Levi Strauss Company identified within the general market of people who buy jeans one specialized market—women willing to pay more money for customized jeans to avoid having to squeeze their unique bodies into standardized, poorly fitting jeans. Levi developed the computer and manufacturing technology to provide jeans custom-made for an individual woman's body. As Martha points out, marketing one to one is great for customer retention. Once a customer's measurements are logged into the Levi computer, she is unlikely to shop elsewhere for jeans, even if jeans are on sale right in her neighborhood.

According to Martha and Don, target marketing is fast becoming a necessity to retain and expand your customer base. It's not enough anymore to satisfy customers—you have to WOW them.

7. Get Inside Your Customer's Head and Learn His Language

When you focus your energies on a target market, you come to understand in far greater depth that market's needs, and how you can provide value. You learn the particular language of the industry in a way that you can't master as an outsider. For example, when I travelled to Puerto Rico after nine years of studying Spanish, I thought I'd be able to converse comfortably with Spanish-speaking natives. My fluency in Spanish turned out to be weaker than I thought. I wasn't familiar enough with the dialect or slang of the country to speak or understand the Spanish spoken so rapidly around me. Studying the language in school was a whole lot different than living in the country and mastering the language in the native environment.

How do you learn the native language of your niche market? Read the publications your customers read; participate in Internet discussion groups; and attend your clients' association meetings. Before I spoke at one network marketing company's national convention, I asked for referrals to local distributors. I met with one and conversed with others by e-mail. I got to know their business and expressions that are unique to their industry. Then, when I wrote my speech, I included terms familiar to the audience, which greatly enhanced my rapport with the group.

Linda Blackman, CSP, is an executive coach, coauthor of *The Sales Coach,* and a sales trainer. She helps her corporate clients deliver more effective presentations. One of her favorite techniques is to show them how to weave into their presentations personal vignettes, sometimes called signature stories, to establish rapport and credibility.

Here's an example she shares about one of her clients, Mark George, a vice president of an environmental company who hired Linda to help him give a presentation about industry innovation:

Mark was having a difficult time trying to figure out how to sell his soon-to-be audience of CEOs and presidents on how exciting this innovation would be to the industry and its customers. I suggested to Mark that we put his talk aside for a moment and just chat about what was going on in his life. He gave me an odd look, asking, "Why?" I replied, "I have an idea. Do you mind if I ask you some questions?" He said no, so I asked.

"What's new with you and your wife?" He told me they had moved recently. His wife was busy with her job, didn't like the shopping mall near the new house, but they loved their new home. Mark said he had spent a fair amount of time at the dentist's office lately to take care of an abscessed tooth. "Oh, speaking of doctors, I just had a baby granddaughter." He smiled, but I detected a bit of concern in his eyes.

I offered my congratulations and asked how his granddaughter was. "Fine now, but she had a rough time in the beginning. They were able to keep her alive with breathing tubes, and it seemed like they used every type of tube imaginable. Just a few years ago, she wouldn't have made it. Today, medical science is incredible, and my granddaughter is beautiful."

Bingo! I found what I needed. A story belonging to Mark that everyone in the audience could relate to, find interesting, and would make the point of how technical know-how could save a life. This story showed how innovations could be life-saving, and it wasn't much of a stretch then to show how the environmental industry's life could depend upon the use of the technological innovation Mark was introducing. The example he used of his granddaughter helped Mark win the critical support of his audience.

Linda helped Mark shape his presentation into a story and language that the audience would respond to with less rejection than if Mark had tried to sell the benefits of innovation forcefully from the start of his presentation.

When you know the specific fears and issues that exist in your market (through market research and experience in the business), you can tailor your message to offer solutions to the problems of most concern to your customers. You can speak in their language, not your own. Your audience will be much less likely to reject you if they see you as an insider, part of the family.

 **TRY THIS!**

Ask one of your best clients to review your sales literature with an eye toward incorporating meaningful industry-specific lingo.

Think of a significant moment in your life that would make a poignant or funny story to share with your clients, to help relax them, establish rapport, or show them that you are one of them. It doesn't even have to be a business story. In fact, sometimes it's better if it isn't.

One morning, I was giving a talk to a group of women with Arbonne International, a network marketing company, at their annual convention in Texas. I had been away from home for a day, and I was missing my babies. My talk was on the topic of balancing work and family. I started off by describing to the audience what it felt like for me to call my young daughters (at that time, ages two and one) to say good morning and I love you, and to hear them refuse to come to the phone because Barney was on TV. I had been replaced by a big purple dinosaur! When I started off my presentation with this quick story, the audience knew that I had experienced some of the same struggles they had, and I wasn't going to give them an academic, theoretical speech. I was walking in their shoes.

IT CAN TAKE A LONG TIME

It takes a long time to penetrate a market (three to five years at least), before you really understand what makes it tick, where people experience frustration, what unmet needs exist, and how your business can fill the gap. If you focus on a niche market long enough, your clients eventually will come to you almost entirely by referral and repeat business. Customers will seek *you* out, and your rejection rate will diminish dramatically.

If you work a particular market actively, and you experience rejection constantly, you may be presenting yourself to the wrong market! Look at the rejection as useful feedback, and refine your approach, your product or services, or your idea of the perfect customer.

If you see positive signs but you aren't profitable as quickly as you'd like to be, look at whether you may just need an extra dose of patience. A profitable business often is not as easy to come by as you think when you first start out. Sometimes it takes a year or two longer to penetrate a market than you imagined it would. You don't want to give up too soon on a market that shows great potential. Self-employed professionals who jump from product to product, switching their emphasis frequently, lose the benefits of establishing themselves as experts in a particular industry. That doesn't mean you shouldn't move on from a target market that turns out to be unprofitable for you. Differentiate between (1) markets that once were profitable but no longer are, (2) markets that aren't profitable yet but show great promise to be profitable over time, and (3) markets that you thought would work but turn out to be duds.

If it turns out that you are doing all the right stuff, and you are focused in the right direction, but it's just taking longer than you'd like, turn to the next chapter, "Stay in the Game," for tips on how to hang in long enough to reap the rewards of your hard work.

Stay in the Game

SHOULD I STAY IN THE GAME?

A business owner who says he has never, even for one minute, doubted whether he is on the right path is lying either to you or to himself. Even entrepreneurs with burning passion in their guts and bulldog persistence have quitting days, when they question their ability, their sanity, and their commitment. Once you go beyond the romance stage, into the nitty gritty of entrepreneurial life, obstacles and rejection appear regularly, and they wear you down from time to time, no matter how determined you are to succeed.

On those difficult days, it's natural to reevaluate your decision to put your self-esteem and your finances on the line in pursuit of an entrepreneurial dream. When Murphy's law seems to be the law of the land, you probably ask yourself: "Am I being tested? Should I keep going, or is this a sign that I'm on the wrong path?" How do you distinguish between rejection that helps you improve, that solidifies and strengthens your commitment and perhaps helps you refine a new, more effective approach to your market, versus rejection that may be alerting you that it's time to look for another way to make a living?

MILEAGE ON THE ODOMETER

The hardest time to cope with rejection is in the beginning years, when you struggle to become profitable and credible and to prove your worth to your family, your community, and especially yourself. You are a baby learning to walk, and rejection can knock you down easily until you and your business have matured and evolving self-confidence and happy, paying, repeat customers make you steadier on your feet.

Greg Jenkins and Tom Neighbors are long-time success-ful business partners and cofounders of Bravo Productions, a Long Beach, Florida, company that produces special effects and props for the movie industry. They introduced me to the concept of mileage on the odometer. Tom says:

We've been in business for ten years. Only in the last four or five years have I come to believe that it will all work out for the best, even if we lose a bid. Because we are a creative team, we can allocate our resources to only a few jobs at any one time. I remember when a client we had produced work for, and given 150 percent of our-selves to in the past, didn't give us the account the fol-lowing year. I was angry, but then something even better came along. It turned out to be a blessing in disguise that we weren't tied up with the former client's project. It allowed us to expand into new areas.

That kind of thing has happened to us many times over the years. It's a matter of mileage on the odometer.

When entrepreneurs first start a business, the mile-age isn't there yet. It's easy to throw in the towel. Now we have had enough years of experience to trust that when we lose a sale, something greater will come around— because we've seen it happen. Entrepreneurs have to hang in there long enough to rack up the miles on the odometer.

Before you read several strategies for *how* to stay in the game, be sure you've answered the question: "*Should* I stay in the game?"

Take the following two quizzes to help you determine whether remaining in your current job, business, or profes-sion makes sense for you. If the answer is yes, the rest of this chapter will tell you how to do that better. If the answer is no, you shouldn't be playing this game anymore, take heart. That doesn't mean that all of your hard work is for naught. It may be time for you to redirect yourself to a different line of work, taking with you all of the valuable lessons you learned in your current endeavor.

QUIZ 1: WHAT IS YOUR RETURN ON INVESTMENT?

It is short-sighted to measure your success by profit alone. You invest your emotional energy and time as well as your dollars, and you receive far more than cash in return. To evaluate whether your current business venture gives you a strong, moderate, or poor return on your investment in emotional satisfaction, take the following quiz.

Score each sentence from 1 to 5 (1—doesn't describe me at all; 2—describes me sometimes; 3—describes me often; 4—describes me most of the time; and 5—describes me almost all of the time).

Total Investment:

1. I invested all of our savings and went heavily into debt to launch my company.
2. We still scrimp personally because profit is much less than we projected at this point.
3. I've taken on enormous responsibility, and I often dread facing it when I wake up.
4. My spouse and/or children defer their material needs to free resources for my business, and they're starting to resent it.
5. I think about my business constantly, even in bed at night.

6. I've foregone other, more lucrative and appealing opportunities to launch this business, and not without some regrets.
7. I go the moon and back for my clients, but I don't feel that they notice.
8. I invest so much time in my business, but it does not have the impact on my field or community that I had hoped for.
9. I've put my business before family, even at crucial times.

Total investment score =

Total Return:

1. Cash flow is stable or comfortable. I am as profitable as my financial obligations require.
2. I love my work and consider it the right livelihood for me.
3. My business allows me flexibility and freedom.
4. My time and money give me the best return I can achieve, personally and financially.
5. I value the personal growth that comes from being self-employed. My business challenges me.
6. My colleagues and customers are fascinating and enjoyable, and they enrich my life.
7. I get satisfaction from the way my product or services improve my customers' lives.
8. It means a lot to me to hear the gratitude my customers express.
9. My business makes it easier for me to balance work, family, and other interests in my life.

Total return score =

Divide your investment score into your return score to determine your return on investment.

If you scored less than 1. Your return on investment is poor. It's time to consider moving on to another livelihood or radically changing the way you do business. You may be profitable and still score less than 1 because profitability isn't the only measure of work satisfaction. Your current business isn't fulfilling.

If you scored between 1 and 3. Your return on investment is moderate. You probably enjoy your work most of the time, but your score is lowered by heavy leveraging in the launch of your business, slow gains in profit, or business troubles that weigh on your mind. If you feel as though you are pursuing the right livelihood for you and making a contribution, you'll likely stick it out until profit increases or until you become accustomed to less income than you would prefer.

If you scored more than 3. Your return on investment is high. Even if you aren't as profitable as you would like, the satisfactions in your work compensate for unstable income. You are unlikely to close your business or move to another line of work unless an act of God or unplanned family circumstances force you to.

The next time you find yourself measuring your success by profitability alone, consider all the rewards of self-employment before you decide to close up shop.

QUIZ 2: WHAT IS YOUR REJECTION THRESHOLD?

Each type of business has its own kinds of rejection that an entrepreneur must endure to be successful. As we discussed in Chapter 3, "Accept Your Limits," each person has limits to what she—and her family—is willing and able to endure to be successful. How much pain do the rejection and customer complaints in your business cause you? Can you handle it? Or is it time to find another profession that will lessen the kind of rejection that troubles you so much?

In the following quiz, score each sentence from 1 to 5 (1—doesn't describe me at all; 2—describes me sometimes; 3—describes me often; 4—describes me most of the time; and 5—describes me almost all of the time).

1. I can't sleep at night because I rehearse mentally how I'll handle rejection tomorrow, or I obsess over how I should have handled rejection better today.

2. To help me cope with my anxiety about rejection, I overeat, undereat, smoke too many cigarettes, drink too much alcohol, or turn to recreational drugs.

3. I'm snappy and short-tempered with my spouse and children because I'm so uptight about the business.

4. I get a sick feeling in my stomach when I have to make sales presentations or cold calls related to my business.

5. I don't seem to be getting any better at handling rejection and criticism in my business, no matter how much sales coaching, training, and practice I give it.

6. I don't enjoy my work.

7. I think every day about how much more successful I would be if only I could delegate all of the sales and marketing in my business to someone else.

8. My self-esteem and self-confidence have plummeted since starting this business.

9. I am not prospering financially in my business.

10. I think almost every day about quitting and finding another way to make a living. I think I'm poorly matched for this profession, and I should cut my losses and move on.

11. I cry most days or feel like doing so.
12. I'm tempted to oversleep because I dread getting up in the morning and facing the day.
13. I know I could get over my fear of rejection if I worked hard enough at it—but I'm not sure I want to suffer that much. The issues are so deeply ingrained, I'd need some serious therapy to get over them. I'd rather find an easier way to make a living.
14. When a customer criticizes me or complains about our product, it unravels me and I don't get much accomplished the rest of the day.
15. I'm ashamed that I let a foolish thing like my fear of rejection get in the way of being successful. I keep trying to pretend it's no big deal, but it really is for me.

If you scored between 60 and 75. It may be time to find another profession. If you experience all of the above emotions most or all of the time, it's very likely that you have been trying to be something you can't. You'd be better off finding a new game instead of focusing on how to stay in this one, especially if your health, sanity, and marriage suffer. No matter what you do for a living, you have to handle rejection. Search for a profession that doesn't push your buttons in such a tortuous way. Lighten up on yourself, and allow for the possibility that this road isn't the one for you. That's okay. You might even be able to remain self-employed or in sales if you find a different kind of sales. For example, switch from consumer to business-to-business sales, or replace face-to-face sales with telephone sales. Just because you have trouble with one form of sales doesn't mean you can't be superb in another.

If you scored between 30 and 59. Rejection challenges you, but you can learn to manage it. If you stay in the game long enough, you likely will succeed; however, you will have days when you are undecided about whether to quit or push on. For most entrepreneurs, there comes a defining moment when they are no longer confused and they know exactly what they need to do.

Here are eight considerations to help you decide whether to continue when you feel discouraged:

1. Consider your health and fatigue level. Do you need a short break, a vacation, or a reprieve from the hours of work, or are you completely exhausted, out of gas, and depleted of all reserves? Is your family worried about your physical state?

2. Consider your spouse's level of support. Is he weary of the sacrifices? Has she become so resentful toward your business that it has created a barrier between you?

3. Consider your family's needs as well as your own. Do your mate and children require you to push on for their sakes, even though you would make different choices if you were single? Are you less emotionally and physically available for your family? Do you sink your family into ever-increasing debt?

4. Consider the enormity of personal growth required of you to surmount your fears and resistance. Are you up for the challenge and willing to do what it takes, even if you'll find it painful?

5. Consider the alternative. Would you rather get a job working for someone else?

6. Consider the scope and magnitude of your challenges. Are you just having a bad day, week, or month, or, after months of discouragement, do you need to face the hard truth that you and this business aren't a good match?

7. Consider environmental and family factors. The morning after a sleepless night or when you suffer from PMS is not a good time to evaluate whether you should continue in your business. Are your blues a result of environmental influences, or are they related directly to your business?

8. Consider the positives as well as the negatives. Do you still receive a regular dose of positive reinforcement along with the challenges? Is there hope on the horizon? Are your profits increasing and your reputation growing, and you just need to be patient? Has it been a long time since running your business was any fun?

If you scored less than 30. You've found a profession that is well-matched for your rejection tolerance. Like any business owner, you have days when a disgruntled customer or disinterested prospect unsettles you, but it doesn't make you question your commitment to your profession or whether you are cut out for the work. You'll stay in the game for as long as it takes to succeed.

TEN STRATEGIES FOR IMPROVING YOUR STAYING POWER

The rest of this chapter assumes that you have decided to give your current venture your full commitment. The following ten strategies will help you improve your staying power:

1. Make it fun.
2. Celebrate small victories along the way.
3. Develop patience and be realistic about the success you hope for.

4. Be accountable to someone or something other than yourself.
5. Be courageous.
6. Keep yourself and your environment healthy.
7. Don't quit too early in the sales process.
8. Stick around even if you don't feel like it.
9. Don't make any major decisions immediately following a rejection.
10. Get your ego stroked outside of your business.

1. MAKE IT FUN

Do you enjoy selling, marketing, and servicing your customers, or are these actions only necessary evils to achieve the profits you desire? If you spend most of your day in activities you don't enjoy and don't do well, chances are you won't stick with your business for long. The promise of prosperity won't be enough incentive for you to spend the majority of your day suffering. When the money arrives, if it does at all, you'll say to yourself: "Is this all that life is about? I want to do something I enjoy!"

The secret to staying in the game for years is to love what you do—all of it (or at least most of it). Maybe you'll never relish dealing with an irate customer who shouts obscenities at you, and some aspects of sales and marketing may trouble you forever, but you'd better have fun interacting with your customers and prospects or you'll burn out quickly. If sales and customer contact aren't your fortes, you may delegate these responsibilities primarily to a partner or employees. However, if you work in a customer-oriented business, and you don't like dealing with customers, rethink your profession. Perhaps you've heard the joke—or is it a true story?—about the medical practitioners who complained that practicing medicine would be much more enjoyable if it weren't for the patients.

 **TRY THIS!**
■ ■ ■

Look for a way to make your business fun. I can't tell you what fun looks like for you. Your idea of an enjoyable activity might be my idea of a nightmare (for example, you won't get me on a roller coaster during this lifetime, but some people stand in line for hours for just that privilege).

The following questions may help you find, or reclaim, the joy in your business:

1. What part of your business would you do even if you weren't paid to do it?
2. What do you love about your work?
3. How do you celebrate small victories and successes?
4. Think of your favorite customer service experience. What made it so rewarding?
5. When do you really enjoy selling your product or services? To whom? Where? How?
6. Do you have fun in your business? If not, why not? What can you do about that?
7. What do you enjoy doing as a hobby? Do you do what you love for a living? If not, would you consider it?

Dealing with rejection isn't fun. Responding to irate customers isn't pleasurable. Keeping up with some of the mundane aspects of running a business can be a drag. So what inspires you to leap out of bed in the morning with a positive outlook on the day—besides the need to pay bills? Find a way, today, to add a bit more fun to your day. This can include time with your spouse, children, and friends as well.   ...!

2. CELEBRATE SMALL VICTORIES ALONG THE WAY

One of the secrets to staying in the game is to set short-term and long-term goals and to stick with them. Every successful businessperson talks about the power of visualizing and writing down goals, then having an action plan to carry them out. I won't belabor that point because you've probably heard it hundreds of times. I'd like to remind you, though, of something just as important to keeping your motivation high and your sensitivity to rejection low: celebrating small victories along the road to success.

Don't wait until you land the big contract, sell the company for a million bucks, or publish the great American novel before you celebrate your achievements. You might never get there if you don't nurture that part of you that needs some positive reinforcement along the way. Mark your simple yet significant accomplishments—those actions that pave the way toward success on a larger scale—on a daily and weekly basis. When you work for a corporation, you are reviewed at least once a year, and if you have a savvy boss, you are praised regularly and appreciated for your daily work. As a self-employed professional, you must learn to give yourself regular encouragement and pats on the back. You also must learn to be grateful for what you have achieved instead of focusing only on what you lack.

For example, when writing a book of this size, it can be tempting to celebrate only when the book reaches bookstores. The problem with this approach, however, is that it can take up to two years for one of my books to move from inception to finished product. It would be very difficult for me to display enthusiasm through the entire process if I didn't stop to celebrate milestones along the way. My many milestones include completing the book proposal; contracting with a major publishing house; completing interviews and research; writing a first draft of the manuscript; having a publishing house accept the manuscript; holding the finished book before it is disseminated to the public; and so on. I pause and appreciate even small accomplishments like scheduling a radio or television appearance or getting an enthusiastic endorsement. Hundreds of small victories add up over a period of years, and sometimes, when I feel impatient for the finished product, it helps to look back at how many obstacles I've already maneuvered successfully.

3. DEVELOP PATIENCE AND BE REALISTIC ABOUT THE SUCCESS YOU HOPE FOR

Imagine you are preparing homemade spaghetti sauce. You place into a pan the choicest tomatoes and spices, combine them gently, then simmer for several hours until the mouthwatering aroma finally beckons you to eat. If you sampled the sauce just after you combined the ingredients, even if they were the finest ingredients money could buy, the sauce would not be appealing. Homemade sauce takes time to season and reach its peak. The same principle applies to profiting in business.

Most successful entrepreneurs aren't overnight sensations, though many enter the scene hoping for such good fortune. When you don't plan realistically for the fact that it takes most business owners three to five years to become profitable, you may become frustrated and give up too soon.

It's fine to hope for easy success, but don't count on it. Most blessings and achievements unfold over time. Good things are worth waiting for.

 **TRY THIS!**

To develop greater patience, recognize the rewards you have received in your life because you were patient. Consider any relationships or experiences of value that you would not have now if you hadn't been patient. Write those awarenesses down, ending with the statement, "It was worth waiting for." Some examples follow:

"My current marriage required patience when I had to wait for my husband's divorce to be finalized. Our marriage was worth waiting for."

"I met my closest friend at a National Speakers convention. She didn't return my phone calls for two months because she was travelling. I'm glad I didn't give up trying to reach her. Our friendship was worth waiting for."

"It took me two years to land the account that finally launched me on the national scene. I'm so glad I didn't give up in the sparse years. My business success was worth waiting for."

"I lost my excess weight slowly over a year's time. I have retained my weight loss for more than ten years. Losing weight slowly and permanently was worth waiting for."

Use whatever opportunity presents itself to strengthen your patience—even for five or ten minutes at a time. Practice patience when it matters least—standing in line at the supermarket checkout, for example. See if you can shift your mental state from irritation and restlessness to serenity and flexibility when the customer in front of you takes out a handful of coupons or the bagger moves so slowly that you'd rather do it yourself. Try driving at the speed limit on the way home from the grocery store.

Once you master patience in short intervals, in situations that scarcely matter, use this new intention and ability in circumstances with higher emotional charges and longer time spans.   ...!

4. BE ACCOUNTABLE TO SOMEONE OR SOMETHING OTHER THAN YOURSELF

To whom or what are you accountable, other than yourself? This person or thing helps you stick it out when the going gets tough. Even so, on some days you feel like packing it in. That's normal!

Rick Gardner is president of Private Party Cars, a Reno, Nevada, company with a novel idea. It provides display space for people who have vehicles for sale and offers financing to help the vehicles sell. Instead of putting an advertisement in the local paper, a customer with a car to sell can park it at Rick's parking lot, where hundreds of car seekers peruse the lot looking for the cars of their dreams. He acts as a matchmaker between sellers and buyers.

Rick has been in business for 15 years, and he now earns a healthy income. It hasn't always been that way, though. When he launched his business, Rick was introducing a new concept to the community. It took four years to make a profit while he earned a solid reputation and gained the trust and respect of his customers. With such a long wait for the cash to show up, you can bet Rick had plenty of days when he thought of packing it all in. But he stuck it out. Why? Because Rick was accountable:

> I had too much of an investment to leave—I couldn't quit. I borrowed money to make it roll. I did try to quit,

though. I quit for three hours the first time. The second time, I walked down the street and waited for my wife to pick me up. That lasted all day. The third time I quit, it lasted only an hour.

Whether you are responsible to a banker, a mortgage, kids needing braces or college, or a family loan, the obligation may prevent you from quitting each time you want to. One of the great differences between being a grown-up and an adolescent is how you respond to responsibilities and obligations in life. Mature adults learn that life isn't always fun. Sometimes you have to do things you'd rather not do to fulfill your commitments.

Hire a business coach or confide your goals in a trusted friend or spouse to help you stay on track. You become accountable to them as well. Speaking your intentions out loud makes it harder to back away when the process gets difficult.

5. BE COURAGEOUS

Sometimes you'll not just step out of your comfort zone when you handle rejection, you'll leap so far away from it, others will shake their heads in amazement or admiration when they witness what you will do to be successful. Staying in the game becomes easier once you have done something outlandish that shifts your business in a positive direction and boosts your self-confidence. When you summon the courage to face your worst nightmare (as outlined in Chapter 1 "Identify the Roots of Your Fear") and you succeed, your fears of rejection often slip away.

Sandra Crowe, author of *Since Strangling Isn't an Option*, shares one of my favorite chutzpah stories in *Chicken Soup for the Soul at Work:*

It was 1986. I had just closed my advertising agency and was close to broke, with no idea as to what to do next. Then one day, after reading a magazine article that talked about the power of networking, a light bulb went off. I would create a company called *Powerlunch!* People seeking contacts would call me, and in the role of business yenta (matchmaker), I would find the exact type of person in the industry they needed, or the exact position they were looking for. Then I'd put the right people together for a power lunch. Perfect, right?

I had very little money to start a business, so I used the one asset that has never failed me—my mouth. I printed 10,000 brochures at an inexpensive local print shop, got up my courage and planted myself on the corner of Connecticut and K Avenues in the middle of downtown Washington, D.C. At the top of my lungs I yelled, "POWERLUNCH! Get your POWERLUNCH!" For three days, I yelled and passed out brochures.

At the end of three days, all the brochures were gone and not one person had called. Penniless, lifeless and beginning to lose hope, I dragged myself home. As I walked in the door, the telephone rang. It was a *Washington Post* reporter. He had seen one of my brochures and wondered if he could interview me to be on the front page of the *Post's* "Style" section. The next day we had a great interview, and he asked me for my business phone number. I told him I would get back to him with it that afternoon. I then scrambled down to the local phone company and called him with the number.

The next day I was awakened by a phone call from a friend congratulating me on the article in the paper. I sat bolt upright in bed. My new phone number hadn't been hooked up yet! Just then, there was a knock on the door. It was the woman from the telephone company, thank goodness. She went to the back of the house to hook me up and emerged after about 15 minutes with a piece of paper. "What's this?" I asked.

"These are the messages I took while I was on the pole," she replied with a laugh.

My business was already one step ahead of me. Many other media sources called. I received hundreds of requests for lunches and introduced many people. It all started on the corner of Connecticut and K, with a lot of yelling . . . and a little bit of courage.

People often view professionals with chutzpah as lucky. After being in the right place at plenty of *wrong* times, they occasionally get "lucky" and are exactly where they need to be when a big break happens.

Wayne Root, author of *The Joy of Failure,* chronicles his climb from an unknown want-to-be-television sportscaster to one of the top sports anchors in the country. Look at how Wayne was able to grab a career-breaking opportunity when he refused to give up, despite a potentially devastating disappointment:

Fox Television executive Michael Binkow invited me to fly to Los Angeles to interview for the host position of a newly proposed national television sports show. I was so sure this was the break I'd been waiting for, I even paid for my friend and mentor, Doug Miller, to fly to Los Angeles with me—to act as my agent. Once I got to Los Angeles, it became clear that this was just another false alarm.

Here I was with my "agent" in Los Angeles, all dressed up with no place to go. I began dialing every television station in Los Angeles. I vowed to turn a wasted cross-country trip and the biggest disappointment of my young career into the biggest break of my life—and I did!

Doug and I sat in our hotel room for two full days waiting for the phone to ring. It never did. At one point, even Doug—the eternal optimist—suggested giving up and heading back home. Instead of [making me] listen to reason, Doug's words inspired and angered me. I made another few hours' worth of phone calls, and one of those calls hit pay dirt.

After more than a year of effort and more than a dozen calls to Arnie Rosenthal, general manager of Financial New Network (FNN) Sports, I decided I had nothing to lose by making one more call. I was shocked when Rosenthal himself actually got on the phone. "Where are you?" he asked. When I told him I was in Los Angeles, his response was like music to my ears: "Wow, what great timing. Our number one anchorman, Todd Donoho, just announced this morning that he's leaving for ABC. How soon can you be here?"

Within an hour, I negotiated a deal that would put me on national television in front of more than 33 million viewers. At the age of 27, I became one of the youngest national television hosts and anchormen ever on a major American television network!

Never give up hope. Sooner or later, if you are on the right path, your lucky break is bound to happen—but only if you keep playing. Your version of chutzpah may look nothing like Sandra's or Wayne's. Maybe for you, chutzpah is simply picking up the phone and cold calling a prospect. A client of mine fantasized about landing her dream account—Bloomingdale's, an upscale retail store in the Northeast. We worked together on one coaching call to help her gather the courage to do one thing: call the contact person for Bloomingdale's who purchased the kind of product she manufactured. I pointed out to her, among other things, that she had nowhere to go but up because at the moment, Bloomingdale's didn't even know she existed. She came to see that the only thing that stood between her and her dream was the act of courage it would take to pick up the phone. It was hard for her, almost excruciating at first, but she did it anyway and was able to proceed toward achieving her dream.

Sometimes, even though you are afraid that other people might judge you, or you run the risk of further disappointment, you must take a leap of faith and do something outrageous. Sometimes you must do what needs to be done.

6. KEEP YOURSELF AND YOUR ENVIRONMENT HEALTHY

To bolster your ability to handle repeated rejection, surround yourself with positive people, and take excellent care of your health. Nothing wears you down faster than disability, fatigue, poor eating habits, too much alcohol, and lack of exercise. Your self-confidence hinges on your sense of inner strength, which often relates to how your body feels.

When you are overworked, it's easy to put such simple tasks as eating well and exercising at the bottom of your to-do list, delaying them until you have more time. Before you know it, you might have plenty of time—when you are bedridden with the flu or your business goes belly up. Therefore, put the hour a day you need to devote to caring for yourself at the top of your priority list.

Along with treating your body well, associate with people who care about you and take good care of you to help you keep your mental condition in top form as well. When you feel low, and business-related rejection is hard to take, lean on at least one friend you can vent to, a spouse who hugs you, or a loyal coach who reminds you of what's great about you. Take a vacation from the naysayers, cynics, and jealous colleagues who resent your success and don't wish you well. Stay clear of anyone who brings you down when you need uplifting the most.

7. DON'T QUIT TOO EARLY IN THE SALES PROCESS

Timing is everything in the business world. Even when you do everything right, you'll be rejected if it's not the right time for your product to reach the hands of the person you prospect.

Hal Becker, author of *Can I Have 5 Minutes of Your Time?*, reports this telling research finding:

> Of all sales, 63% are made after the fifth rejection. That means you need to hear five nos before you hear a yes from a prospect.
>
> But 75% of all salespeople give up after their first rejection.
>
> That explains why 25% of the sales forces often produces 95% of the results. Every day, thousands of sales are made to customers who previously said no.

We've all seen small miracles—special coincidences and acts of fate that turn the hand you're dealt into a winner in the last round. If you give up too soon, you won't experience this "lucky" turnaround.

Also, some customers say no many times before they finally say yes. When you experience that phenomenon often enough, you learn how to hear those first few noes as "no, not at this time" rather than "no, not *ever!*"

"HE STARTED OUT AS A TINY SEED OF DOUBT."

Pam Lontos, a national sales trainer, helps salespeople understand the buyer's psyche so that they can see that saying no may be, ironically, just a necessary step in the process of saying yes. Here's what she teaches her clients:

People say no because they are afraid of making a decision. They may very well want what you are selling.

People have a certain number of noes they have to say before they feel safe saying yes. Until they feel confident making the decision to say yes, prospects will give you false objections and even lie. "No" means "Tell me more—I'm not convinced enough to say yes." It doesn't necessarily mean "I don't want it."

"No" often is phrased in these frequently heard objections:

"I don't have the money."

"I tried it once, and it didn't work."

"I have to talk to my partner."

The only way around these rejections is to excite the prospects' interest right from the start. If you convince them up front that there is a benefit to listening to you, you will be given a chance to talk.

The more benefits you give, the more you will raise the prospects' desire to want to buy.

Finally, when the desire is high enough, the fear of making a decision will leave. Their subconscious minds will say, "I've said no X number of times, and it still looks good, so I guess it's okay to say yes." Each person has a different number of noes he has to go through. If you are talking to a 6-no person and you stop at the fifth no, you were just one more no away from getting the sale!

We tend to focus on our own fears of rejection, not considering that a prospect expresses her fears at the same time. Take your focus off of protecting yourself, and shift your attention to reassuring your prospective customer. Sometimes "no" doesn't mean "no, not now, not anytime, not ever—go away!" but rather "I'm afraid of making the wrong decision. Can you help me?"

 **TRY THIS!**
■ ■ ■

Get inside your customer's head for a moment. What is he afraid of? If he doesn't buy from you right away, what wrong decision is the customer afraid of making? Think about what you can say during your sales presentation to help allay those fears.   ■ ■ ■ **!**

8. STICK AROUND EVEN IF YOU DON'T FEEL LIKE IT

When you recite your marriage vows, you acknowledge up front that you may have days when you feel like leaving, but you won't because you made a life-long commitment to your spouse—for better and for worse. You'll have times in your marriage, as anyone does, when you can't stand your spouse and when you fantasize about how much better your life would be if he or she changed. You'll wish sometimes that you could trade in your mate for a new model. If you are committed to your marriage, however, you won't act on these fantasies. You'll stick it out, even when you experience some difficult times.

Sometimes staying in business isn't fun, isn't easy, isn't what you really want to do. You'd rather run. You'd rather do something else. You want to cry, or scream, or go to sleep and not think about it at all. But you get up the next morning and do it all again because you made a commitment—to yourself, to your spouse, to your employees, to your customers, to those who depend on you to fulfill your mission. Be willing to suffer—not all of the time (if so, you are in the wrong business) but at least some of the time—if that is what it takes to honor your commitments.

 **TRY THIS!**
■ ■ ■

Think about this question: To what and whom are you committed enough to suffer through painful rejection and difficult working experiences?   ■ ■ ■ !

9. DON'T MAKE ANY MAJOR DECISIONS IMMEDIATELY FOLLOWING A REJECTION

Published romance author Katherine Garbera has learned to take rejection letters in stride. After receiving one, she gives herself some time to rant and be depressed, then she learns from the rejection and moves on, making necessary changes to the book or starting a new project. Following is her sage advice to authors who struggle with the rejection inherent in the publishing process. Her words apply to anyone who receives a painful rejection:

> First, put the letter aside, and don't look at it again for at least a week. Give yourself a pep talk, and call that one friend who knows you and your writing and who'll cheer you up. Someone who will commiserate with you on the rejection and help you get through it. This is not the time to call a friend or relative who is not a writer. They don't get it. They won't understand how you can be so upset by a letter from a faceless person in New York. One writer I know burns her rejection letters. I make a copy and then put it through the shredder.
>
> Second, pick the letter up again after you've cooled off. Look at it objectively. Notice the things you missed the first time—they liked the writing style and the pacing, but the character development was off. The editor may have even offered you some suggestion on why the character didn't develop. Call that writer friend or your agent or someone who can help you brainstorm [about] how to solve these problems.
>
> Third, make changes to the manuscript if that's something you feel comfortable doing, or don't if you feel the changes hurt the integrity of the book. Then send it off again. The only way to sell your book is to send it out.

Fourth, start a new project. Keep in mind the comments that you received in that letter, and use that as a learning tool. Remember why you started writing. Nothing cures the blues like doing what you love to do.

I had the opportunity to heed my own advice about staying in the game while writing this chapter. Even though I consider myself a fairly upbeat, optimistic person, this was a particularly hard month.

A series of major computer problems put me out of commission over a three-week period and left me feeling vulnerable and frustrated. My husband was preoccupied with long working hours, two hours of commuting a day, a moonlight consulting contract, and an active gardening hobby that occupied most of his weekend hours. He and I were spending little time together, and I missed his company and affection. My three babies younger than four had mastered the irritating art of whining, and my newborn wanted to nurse every hour and a half. Against this backdrop, I was getting little sleep, I was up against a tight deadline for completing this book, my summer babysitter quit a month earlier than expected, and then . . .

One day, I logged onto e-mail at 6:00 AM to read the subject "BAD NEWS" from a prospective client who was supposed to be giving me good news. A lucrative consulting contract I was excited about fell through at the last minute, as the final decision maker resigned from the company unexpectedly. Without his support, the deal evaporated. That same day, an envelope arrived from my literary agent filled with rejection letters related to her efforts to sell my next book.

The tears began to flow. My head filled with negative thoughts: "My profession is filled with so many last-minute disappointments, I can't stand it anymore. Rejection after rejection! Why did I have to pick this kind of work? Here I

am, the expert on rejection, and look at me, I'm a mess. Ha!
I can't handle rejection at all. Who am I kidding?"

For a few hours, I felt despondent and fed up. I know not
to make decisions of any magnitude when I'm feeling blue,
so I put aside my normal writing schedule and focused on
answering e-mail and doing busy work that didn't require
the commitment of my heart. I distracted myself with household chores. I played with my newborn, Elijah. I knew that
if I waited a few hours or days, held on to my hope, and stayed
in the game, my optimistic spirit would return.

Sure enough, within a few days, my computer problems
were fixed, my agent had received interest from a publisher
for my next book, and I was on my way to opening up new
opportunities to replace the income I lost from the contract
that failed to materialize.

When you receive some bad news, tread water until you
emerge from whatever funk or negative cycle you may fall in.
"This too shall pass" is the mantra for these times. Keep busy,
talk to a friend, pray, and believe that good times *will* follow
bad. If your depression continues for too long, it may be a
sign that you *should* make some major changes, but take
some space between when you receive a difficult rejection,
and making any significant changes in response to it.

10. GET YOUR EGO STROKED OUTSIDE OF YOUR BUSINESS

Alex Von Allmen, cofounder of Logolabs and a professional logo designer, told me:

> I pour my heart and soul into a logo design, and I
> know it's good. Then a client says, "I was hoping for some-
> thing more creative." I say to myself, "I can't believe they

didn't get how brilliant this is." The client may have a taste that is inappropriate for their market. But you try to give them what they want. I've learned to detach myself and to stop trying to get my artistic fulfillment from my logo design.

Entrepreneurs who provide an artistic product that comes right out of their soul find it nearly impossible to receive rejection without personalizing it (of course, it *is* personal). Writers, artists, playwrights, graphic designers, architects, musicians, photographers, interior decorators and many other professionals have reported feeling devastated by a client or prospective client's rejection. When a prospect turns them down or a client and the media criticizes their work, they question their talents, and it rocks their self-confidence for a period of time.

Those who suggest that you should simply learn not to take it personally don't understand what it feels like to submit yourself—your soul—to the world for review. Yes, customers have different preferences, regardless of your talent, but as an author, I know that it's extremely difficult not to take rejection of your creative work personally. If I am a manufacturers' representative selling windows, and a prospect turns me down, I regret not making the sale. However, I don't internalize the rejection the same way I do when I sell a product that I created.

You can use two strategies to handle this kind of rejection. First, as I mentioned earlier, create a fan mail folder, where you place all of the kudos you've received about your work over time. Frame a particularly positive public review or customer letter, and hang it on the wall. Tape an inspirational saying to the top of your desk. Place a complimentary e-mail on top of your computer so that you can read it regularly. Ask satisfied customers to write you letters of recommendation. Even if you don't need these letters for prospective clients, you'll benefit from them when you feel discouraged. Over time, as your collection of positive communications builds, you won't be knocked over so easily when someone doesn't like your work because you'll remember, and see evidence of, your delighted customers.

Second, find a way outside of your normal course of business to receive the positive feedback you long for. Volunteer at a nursing home, hospital, school, or church. Use your expertise to teach patients, children, or neighbors. Give your product or services away to those who appreciate them, but can't afford to pay. Create a place in your life where your artistic talent and achievement are appreciated by those who aren't buying your product or services so that you can separate recognition of your talent from the business of selling it.

STAY IN THE GAME

If business is like a baseball game, perhaps you'll get lucky and hit a home run with the bases loaded early in the game. Or you may try anxiously to get a runner on base for eight or nine innings and, in the final moments, hit a triple that brings in the game's winning run. Or you may deliver single-base and double-base hits for the entire nine innings, racking up the runs slowly but surely. Regardless of how, when, and how often you hit the ball, you could win the game unless . . . you stop playing before the ninth inning ends. Your obligation is to finish nine innings. If you walk off the field in frustration or fatigue before then, you lose, regardless of how you've played the game so far.

Finish out your game. See it through to the end. Don't let a little rain, a strike-out, or a little rejection stop you from building your field of dreams.

CHAPTER 9

Turn Customer Complaints into Opportunities

Complaints are a form of rejection. They elicit feelings of anger, depression, and hopelessness. They cause us to ask: "Will I ever be good enough?" Complaints hurt. We do the best job we know how, and some customers still aren't happy. We commit a slight error, and a customer makes a federal case of it. We bend over backwards to resolve a customer problem, and the customer continues to be dissatisfied. Complaints are joy busters.

As a business owner, you have no choice but to learn how to take complaints in stride. Experts point out that most industries never do better than to fully satisfy 80 to 82 percent of their customers. *In other words, no matter how superlative your business practices, 18 to 20 percent of your customers will be dissatisfied on average!* Sometimes their dissatisfaction is because of something entirely out of your control.

Greg Jenkins, from Bravo Productions, shares this memory:

> I remember once we built a float for the Rose Parade, based on the color yellow, because that's what the client asked for. We gave the client exactly what they were looking for, and they were happy. Then, we overheard one of the judges saying, "Ugh. I hate the color yellow!" We knew we weren't going to score any points with this judge, regardless of how great the float was!

Sometimes the judge doesn't like yellow. You didn't do a thing wrong and had no way to know about it ahead of time. Human beings have individual preferences and needs, and you won't always be aligned perfectly with every customer, no matter how hard you try. You can be depressed about that reality, or you can release yourself from unrealistic standards of perfection. Complaints come with being self-employed as much as rejection occurs in the sales process.

WHY TAKE COMPLAINTS SERIOUSLY?

Why take complaints seriously? This is a fair question. I could suggest that you lighten up about complaints, ignore them, don't worry about them, focus your energies on your happy customers. That would make your business more enjoyable, right? Some form of detachment is imperative, but you won't be in business long if you ignore your unhappy customers. Several research studies report the same finding.

Dissatisfied customers tell between eight and ten people about the bad service they received. Twenty percent of the dissatisfied customers who vocalize their bad experience to others tell 20 people or more. Now that we have the Internet, an unhappy customer can broadcast his complaint to hundreds, if not thousands, of strangers at a time through discussion lists, bulletin boards, e-mail newsletters, and other cyberspace forums. People who hear of a bad experience retell that experience in their circles of influence, compounding the negative publicity.

I participate actively in a discussion list of authors and publishers. The list includes more than 1,000 names, and every day someone posts a warning to the list about a negative experience she had with a particular business or business professional. Subscribers to the list pay close attention to these postings. At one time, so many people posted a warning about a disreputable radio station that the radio station sent a threatening letter from its lawyers demanding that the postings cease because the radio station was very concerned about the impact of such far-reaching negative publicity.

The Technical Assistance Research Programs (TARP), the most widely quoted research group that focuses on complaining customers, found that 26 out of 27 people who experience poor service do not complain to the company or demand that the company do anything to resolve their dissatisfaction.

Do not assume that a lack of complaints in your business means that everyone is happy. Remember the research I shared earlier—up to 20 percent of your customers probably are dissatisfied, but most of them don't tell you about it.

You have no control over those who simply stop being customers and walk away quietly but then broadcast to the world their bitterness about you and your company. So although customer complaints are difficult to handle at times, bless the complainer for giving you the opportunity to retain him as a customer and to convert his hostility into positive publicity.

Research shows that when a customer complaint is resolved satisfactorily, the customer tells even more people about the successful resolution of her problem than she would have if she had received good service in the first place!

Customer complaints are a gift, even though they make us uncomfortable, and most of us would eliminate them if we could.

The most common tendency is to react defensively, making the customer wrong so that we can make ourselves right. The more sensitive you are to rejection, the more you'll overreact to accusations from a dissatisfied customer. Winning the argument may make your ego feel a little better, but you might lose a customer. Successful business owners learn how to quiet their instinct to argue and replace it with a strategic response that calms the angry customer. Then you can move to convert the customer's anger to satisfaction.

First let's look at how to calm an irate customer. Until the customer can speak reasonably about his concerns, however, it's impossible to progress toward a resolution.

CALMING AN IRATE CUSTOMER

1. Keep Calm

Rebecca Zenk owns Becca's Color Your Own Ceramics, a California company that provides a pleasant atmosphere for people of all ages to create their own ceramic pieces. Artistic customers can get quite emotional about their artwork. Rebecca reports that she spends a good deal of time putting out fires—and we're not talking about fires in the kiln! She's been in the business since 1994, so she's learned a few tricks:

> Here's a typical scenario: A customer spends four hours working on a platter. We do our best to fire it as carefully as possible. Ninety-eight percent of what we fire comes out better than they expected. The other 2 percent—the clay isn't perfect, and it cracks in the kiln. He or she screams: "Why did you do this? How could you let this happen?" Even though the customer creates his or her own work, when it doesn't come out well, it's always our fault.
>
> It used to ruin my day—my blood would boil like theirs. Now, I find it comical, and I have to try hard not to laugh. This is what I've learned:
>
> Don't match their energy—stay calm. I just tell them, "We fire as slow and safe as possible. Clay is imperfect; it comes from the ground. It's the nature of ceramics that things break. You can do it again at no charge, or I'll give you a refund if you don't wish to come back to the studio."
>
> Reasonable customers normally make reasonable demands. Some people aren't worth trying to keep as customers. They're just looking for a fight. Some people just have to be mad at somebody. When I see a customer like

that, I call it the "wacko factor." I don't let it make me crazy anymore.

2. *Let the Customer Vent*

Allow a customer to vent her frustrations completely instead of rushing to fix the problem or to defend yourself. By the time customers are angry enough to complain, they need to vent before they will hear what you have to say. Sometimes venting and receiving an empathetic response are all they really want.

J.J. Lauderbaugh, a customer service consultant and professional speaker, recommends that you rely on the three proven phrases below while an irate customer vents his complaint. These responses allow you to buy time, show respect, make the customer right, and give the customer his dignity:

"I agree with what you are saying."
"I understand that this has inconvenienced you."
"Tell me more about it." (Don't ever say "the problem.")

Here's a caution: Never tell a customer she didn't experience what she reports she experienced. The customer's reality is true for her, whether or not you agree with it. If you try to convince an agitated customer that her experience never happened, you'll just agitate her further.

It's difficult to not feel defensive when a customer complains. Doug Erickson, president of Capitol Modular, Inc., a building supplier and commercial contractor, introduced me to the term "But-I calls":

"But-I" calls are when all you get to say is "But-I" because you are defending yourself. Don't respond that way when a client is really hot. Let him vent. If a customer calls because he wants something fixed, he wants to tell someone about it. He won't get a catharsis if you don't hear him out. [When it's all over,] you want the customer to say, "They really understood my problem, heard what I had to say, and then they fixed it."

Raman Chauhan, founder of Himalayan Hemp, a manufacturer, importer, exporter, and wholesaler of handcrafted hemp products, shares his secret for staying calm when a customer or an employee rants and raves:

> Do you remember when you were 12 years old—you couldn't hear when your mom told you to turn the television off, but you always heard when dinner was ready?
>
> No matter who is complaining to me—a customer, an employee, whoever—I let him vent, and I listen intelligently. I would go nuts if I really listened closely to people whining and complaining all day long. They aren't talking rationally. Until they are done venting, I become like a 12-year-old boy. I selectively check in and then tune them out until they are done venting. Then we can speak together in a calm manner.

The key to Raman's strategy is to tune into the details so you get the picture right, without necessarily focusing on the nasty words and angry tirades that some customers need to express. Sometimes, though, a customer is so vicious, obscene, and unreasonable that you can't get anywhere with him, and you don't want to subject yourself to the abuse.

Kelley Lutz has been working at Lancaster County's credit bureau for more than 25 years. Over the past two decades, she has encountered hundreds of irate customers who blame the credit bureau for problems on their credit reports. When she receives a call from a customer who screams and curses, she waits for a moment of opportunity, then replies calmly, "When you can talk to me civilly, call me back. I'd be glad to help you."

It's easier for Kelley to hang up on or dismiss an irate customer than it may be for you if the person on the other end of the phone or sitting in front of you is a paying customer. Still, you must limit how much abuse you will tolerate from an unhappy customer. Hopefully, allowing the customer a little time to vent will calm her down enough to have a civil conversation. But remember the wacko factor. Some people will be impossible to satisfy, and it's not your fault.

3. Pause and Breathe

When you are attacked, you instinctively hold your breath as adrenaline surges through your body. You prepare yourself for defense, as if a large bear were chasing you. Your body doesn't know the difference between psychological and physical attack. After the dissatisfied customer finishes talking for the moment, pause and breathe before you respond. At first, the pause may seem like an eternity, but it lasts only a few seconds. Pausing and breathing help prevent you from interrupting the customer before he is finished speaking, plus they calm your energy and help you collect your thoughts.

4. Ask Questions

Ask plenty of questions to help you get the details straight. When you think you understand the full complaint, summarize what you believe the customer is unhappy about, then ask whether he wants to add anything else. Thank the customer for bringing the problem to your attention. (To feel really sincere about your gratefulness, remember those hostile customers who don't give you an opportunity to turn around the problem.) Make sure you are clear about exactly what the customer is complaining about before you try to remedy the situation. If you rush this process, the customer will remain dissatisfied because your solution won't address her real concern.

5. Apologize

You may wonder why I suggest you apologize *after* you ask questions. When a customer is angry with you, shouldn't you apologize immediately? In truth, sometimes a quick apology can backfire on you. If the customer hasn't had a chance to explain the details fully, you can't be sure what you are apologizing for, and the customer knows that. Your reflexive apology can come across as a rehearsed response rather than a sincere expression of regret. Try not to begin with an apology, but be sure to weave it into the conversation a bit later. Even if you believe that the customer is at fault and is being unreasonable, you always can say sincerely, "I am sorry that you are so unhappy with your purchase" or "I'm sorry that you are so angry." You can be sorry that an event happened, whether or not you accept the blame for it.

When you've calmed the customer and understand the nature of the problem, it's time to move toward solving it.

CONVERTING AN ANGRY CUSTOMER TO A DELIGHTED ONE—RECOVERY

In late July 1997, my husband, Stephen, and I parted with $250 of hard-earned cash to get our home air ducts cleaned. Our house was 15 years old, and the heating and ventilating system had never been serviced. It had been on our to-do list since we purchased the home. When we stumbled across a $50 coupon for a local cleaning service, we scheduled the work.

Jeff, the general manager, was in our home for two hours with all his pipes, hoses, and machinery. When he announced that he was finished, I wrote him a check for the full amount and thanked him for his time. Later that evening, Stephen came storming down the stairs. Stephen normally is a very even-tempered man. One of the few things that really riles him is feeling that he has been cheated by a service or repair person. Stephen fumed, "What did that guy actually do today?" I replied, "I have no idea. I didn't follow him around the house. He said he cleaned all the ducts."

Well, my detail-oriented and frugal husband had inspected each duct with a flashlight to be sure he was getting good value for his money. Good thing he did! Stephen was furious to discover that the ducts looked little cleaner than they had before the visit. And several of the ducts hadn't been touched at all, although we paid to have all of the ducts in our house cleaned. Because we had paid by check, not credit card, we were vulnerable to being taken advantage of by an unscrupulous company we knew nothing about.

I called the company the next morning and spoke to Jeff, the man who had done the work. He expressed great surprise and concern and scheduled a return trip to our home the following day. Jeff could have said, "Too bad. That's the best we can do"; he already had our check. But as we came to learn, Jeff knows how to treat a customer.

The afternoon Jeff was scheduled to return to our house, a tractor-trailer overturned, spilling 1,000 gallons of liquid asphalt on the highway and grinding traffic to a halt. Jeff called me an hour before he was supposed to arrive at my home to warn me that the accident would slow him down and delay his arrival. He had a reasonable excuse to post-pone until the following day, but he didn't suggest changing the schedule. I was thinking that if he didn't do an accept-able job of remedying the problem, we could still stop pay-ment on the check, so I didn't suggest rescheduling, either.

Two and a half hours later, Jeff finally arrived at our house. He had spent most of that time sitting in traffic. My husband had prepared a list of all of the ducts he questioned, but after glancing at the first one, Jeff replied, "We tried a new way of cleaning ducts at the beginning of this week. Obvi-ously, it didn't work. I should have caught that before I left, and I didn't. I'm sorry. I will reclean every duct in your house."

He continued, "And to make up for the inconvenience, you can call me every year for the rest of the time you live in this house. As long as I'm still in business, I'll clean your ducts again for free."

Jeff's offer was generous and more than we would have asked for or expected. He proceeded to reclean all the ducts in the house. After the job was done, he thanked me for call-ing and telling him of the problem. He then stated, "You are the only customer who called to complain since we started using the new system at the beginning of this week. I'm go-ing to call all of the other customers and alert them to the problem. If they aren't satisfied, I'll go back to their homes and reclean their ducts as well."

Jeff understands how to create a lifetime customer and a book of referrals out of a customer he nearly lost. Because ducts usually are cleaned only every two or three years, he could have said to himself, "Why should I go out of my way to satisfy this customer? She won't be a repeat customer for years, if ever." But Jeff understands the power of both posi-tive and negative word of mouth. He understands that as a dissatisfied customer, I would have spread the word to my circle of influence to stay far away from his company. I even might have been angry enough to report the incident to the Better Business Bureau.

As a delighted customer—even more than a satisfied one—I likely will continue to tell this story about a duct-cleaning business that offered superior customer service. I wrote about it in my syndicated column, "Advice from A–Z," and I'm telling the story again here. You can't pay for that kind of advertising. The original mistake is largely forgotten and entirely forgiven, replaced by admiration for Jeff's approach to remedying the problem.

Therein lies one of the greatest secrets to handling complaints well. Mistakes always happen. It's how you respond to them that matters. When treated right—or even better than right—a dissatisfied customer becomes your best ambassador.

Pamela Demarast, owner of Launder Dog, a California self-service pet wash and professional grooming shop, says it simply: "Don't step over a dollar to get to a dime. You're building relationships with life-time customers." With that perspective, you'll be generous in your attempts to please a dissatisfied customer, even if it loses you money in the short term.

Ron Zemke, author of *Delivering Knock Your Socks Off Service*, reports:

> Most customers only want what they were denied, and perhaps an apology. So if a company gives them a token of atonement beyond what they expected, they will likely reciprocate by continuing to do business and saying positive things about the company. In the hotel industry, researchers have found that the way complaints are handled is the major factor determining whether someone will return for another night's stay.
>
> Companies can create this feeling of reciprocity by taking the customer complaint seriously and offering one or more of the following:

a price reduction, or no charge at all

a sincere apology

a free product or gift

a coupon for future price reductions

assurance that something has been changed inside the
company so that this will not happen again.

Tom Wischmeyer is director and owner of The Golf University, located in San Diego, California. The founder of the school is Ken Blanchard, author of *One Minute Manager.* Tom bought a licensing agreement from him to operate the school. Tom shares two stories that demonstrate how customer mishaps can be great business opportunities:

> I'll never forget the time someone stole a husband's and wife's clubs. We calmed them down right away by telling them, "Look, we're going to make everything okay. You are going to leave here happy. What is it going to take for us to do that?" They replied, "Certainly, we want our clubs replaced." "Of course. What else?" We got them new clubs custom-fitted before they left and gave them a free room and meals. They couldn't say enough about their stay here. We lost money on them, but they have told so many people about us, it has come back to us tenfold.
>
> Another time, I was on the road with Ken Blanchard, and we were awakened by a middle-of-the-night fire alarm in a Sacramento hotel. Turns out, it was a false alarm. The next morning, Ken was appalled that they didn't offer everyone in the hotel a free breakfast. When he was in the dining room for breakfast, he approached the manager and said, "You have a chance to become a hero. Don't waste the opportunity!"

Successful business owners seize the occasion to convert an unhappy customer into a thrilled customer—they even delight in doing so. David Goldsmith, a customer service consultant warns, "If you're going to bother to make a recovery effort, do it well. You can cause more ill will than good if you think 'something' is better than 'nothing!'"

The next time you wonder how far to go to make a customer happy, remember how much it costs to buy advertising for your firm. *You can't buy the kind of positive publicity that a happy customer generates for you.*

IS IT EVER OKAY TO IGNORE A CUSTOMER'S COMPLAINT?

Differentiate between ignoring a customer's complaint and choosing not to change one of your practices just because a customer is not satisfied. You can communicate a willingness to listen and consider a client's request for change without necessarily changing anything.

C. Leslie Charles, author of *The Customer Service Companion,* offers these helpful phrases for communicating a service attitude to your customers:

- "How may I help you?"
- "I'm happy to help."
- "I am unable to do that, but here's what I can do."
- "Thank you for taking the time to let me know."
- "Let's see what we can do."
- "We had no idea a customer might get that impression."
- "I don't know the answers right now, but I'd be happy to find out for you."

But what if a customer has an unreasonable complaint or criticism? Perhaps your product or services never will make her happy. Rather than reshaping yourself to accommodate every customer's complaint, the best thing to do is to let some customers go. Your sensitivity to rejection may tempt you to try to please every customer, and that's a noble goal. Realistically, however, some unhappy customers will drain so much of your energy, you are better off allowing them to take their business elsewhere.

Let's finish this chapter by looking at how you can determine when a criticism is valid and offers useful feedback, and when you may reach the conclusion that this customer will be better served by someone else.

DEFINE YOUR STANDARDS

One morning, after I sent out my bimonthly online newsletter for entrepreneurial couples, I opened an e-mail message from a particularly devoted reader. I was disturbed to read, "I just read the most recent newsletter. It isn't up to your standards." Reading further, I learned that she had not experienced the humor and helpful tips she was accustomed to receiving from my newsletter, and she was disappointed in me.

My reflexive response was to feel hurt, shame, and fear. The mental noise began immediately: "Maybe this issue isn't any good at all. What if everyone on the newsletter list—a few thousand people—feels the same way? Gee, I remember offering lots of helpful tips—what is she talking about?" I re-read her critique carefully, then examined the newsletter. Had I fallen short in a larger way that I needed to pay attention to, or did I simply fail to meet this woman's preferences and needs in this particular issue?

It turns out, due to a cyberspace glitch, she received only half of the newsletter. This woman assumed I had done a poor job in composing the newsletter, but once she received the complete version, she was satisfied. It's a good thing I didn't overreact and revise my newsletter format based only on her criticism.

Professional associations demand compliance with ethical standards of behavior. Other than that, as a self-employed professional, you set expectations of yourself, then develop your own standards for excellence. You aim to ensure that you satisfy your customers' standards, but the most important test is whether you meet your own.

 **TRY THIS!**

To determine whether to change your practices because someone criticizes your work, ask yourself these ten questions:

1. Are the customer's expectations of me reasonable, and can I meet them?
2. Did I fall short of my own expectations and demands for delivering a quality product? Did I give this product or project less than my best?
3. Is the criticism I receive consistent over time? Does it come from more than one person? What percentage of my customers have given me the same kind of feedback?
4. Is the person who delivers the criticism knowledgeable? Do I respect and trust his opinion?
5. Does this person have my best interests at heart, or is it someone who could benefit from tearing me down?
6. How easy is it to make the change being requested?
7. Do I believe that the quality of my product or services will be improved for others if I respond to this customer's feedback?
8. If I change something to satisfy this customer, will I be a traitor to my own standards for success?

9. Do I suspect that this criticism really isn't about me or my product at all but mostly a projection of the customer's unhappiness with herself or some other aspect of her life?
10. How important to my business is it for me to respond to this criticism or to make this customer happy? Is this a customer I want to be sure to satisfy?   ....**!**

You must balance self-confidence and solid vision with flexibility and the willingness to learn from mistakes and improve. Lean too far in either direction, and you are in trouble. Close yourself off from critical feedback, and your business will stagnate. Allow every piece of criticism to make you question your value and self-worth, and you'll have trouble standing your ground when it's important to do so.

LETTING GO OF THE STRESSFUL CLIENT

We discussed in Chapter 7 the importance of focusing your efforts and letting go of clients and prospects who do not fall within your target market and are unlikely to offer a good return on investment of your scarce time and resources. This section looks at a slightly different issue—letting go of customers who may fit your target market profile perfectly (and even pay you well) but who are so difficult to please that you are better off letting them become someone else's problem.

It's extremely difficult to turn away a customer. It's hard to reject any customer who can help you pay the bills. It's difficult to accept that you may not be able to please everyone. So accustomed are you to worrying about being rejected, it may be awkward for you to act the role of rejector. You are apt to try for a very long time to make a customer relationship work before finally giving up. But here's what

customer service experts and business owners say time and again:

When a self-employed professional lets go of a customer who causes him great stress, the business usually grows substantially as the owner's energy becomes freed to pursue new opportunities and to better serve his other clients.

Eva Rosenberg, a tax professional, writer, and speaker located in Encino, California, shares this classic experience:

> After more than 20 years of bending over backwards to help, I've come to the conclusion (and reached the position in life) that I will "fire" a client who causes me stress. In 1995, I took a chance and fired someone who paid me more than $2,000 per year (plus a couple of smaller clients). My income went up by more than 50 percent. In 1996, I dropped about another $5,000 worth of irritations, and my income went up another 25 percent.

It is important to distinguish between a demanding client who causes you too much stress and a client who delivers constructive criticism that is difficult for you to hear. Sometimes it's easier to run from the source than to listen and learn from what a disgruntled customer has to say.

 **TRY THIS!**

Here's a self-assessment tool that will help you determine whether it's time to let a customer go:

1. Whenever I interact with this customer, I feel stressed and tense.
   _____Yes   _____No

2. I would ignore or avoid this customer if I could.
   ____Yes   ____No
3. I've spent many hours trying to make this customer satisfied, but it doesn't seem to be good enough.
   ____Yes   ____No
4. I usually feel worse about myself after speaking with this customer.
   ____Yes   ____No
5. I believe that if I wasn't spending so much time and energy trying to please this customer, I'd be better able to help other customers and prospect for new ones.
   ____Yes   ____No
6. I don't hold a great deal of respect for this customer's critical feedback. I don't feel as if I learn anything helpful from her criticism.
   ____Yes   ____No
7. This is the kind of customer who seems to be negative about everything. I don't think I ever will find a way to make him happy.
   ____Yes   ____No
8. This customer's complaints are inconsistent with feedback I receive from my other customers.
   ____Yes   ____No
9. This customer asks far too much time from me, considering what she pays me.
   ____Yes   ____No
10. I spend too much time outside of work ruminating about this customer. It bothers me at night and lowers my mood when I'm around my spouse and family.
    ____Yes   ____No

If you answered yes to several of these questions, it might be time to write a letter like the following one, used by Nancy Roebke, executive director of Profnet, a networking company, when she decided to end an untenable relationship:

Dear Sir,

It has become apparent to me that we cannot reach a mutually beneficial agreement. Because I value you as a fellow business professional, I feel it is in your best interest that you find another supplier for the services you need. Feel free to use the information my firm has shared with you, if it meets your goals.

Respectfully,

Nancy Roebke

THE ECHO EFFECT OF HANDLING CRITICISM POORLY

We've looked at why it's important to your business success to be able to handle customer complaints well. Let's end this chapter with a reminder of another powerful reason for learning how to handle the rejection and criticism that our customers and prospects deliver: the impact on your family.

When you are rattled by a customer interaction, you probably take it out on your spouse and family to some extent. It might show up as impatience, a short temper, distraction, or emotional absence. Because criticism is so painful for most of us to tolerate, it is nearly impossible to confine our emotional response to criticism to the office. The effects of negative interactions at work echo in our homes as well. We become overly sensitive to criticism from our spouse when we are reeling from criticism at work. We expect too much of our children when we project onto them our own need to deliver a better performance.

Pay attention to how your response to criticism and rejection shows up in your home life. If you find it difficult to shake off unpleasant interactions with customers, devise a way to put some space between you and your work when you interact with your family. Perhaps you'll work out at the gym before heading home for dinner or use the commute time to listen to a motivational audiotape. Maybe just sitting for a half-hour in the sauna at the gym is what you need to relax.

If you notice that you are taking out a lousy mood on your family, stop yourself and apologize, then and there. It takes great self-discipline to keep professional difficulties from spilling over into your family relationships. Work at it diligently, and it will become easier over time. You can stop the echo effect of rejection and criticism. The first step is to open your awareness to how often it happens, then to take responsibility for the true source of your irritation.

Handling criticism is painful. Nothing I can teach you in this book will change the basic fact that most of us don't like to be criticized and never will. If we could find a way to perfect ourselves and our businesses so that every customer is delighted, and we never have to suffer the rejection of an unhappy client, we would earn millions teaching that secret to others. The truth is, as long as you are a human being dealing with other human beings, you will be criticized and rejected. But you can learn to take it in stride, which is what this book is all about.

Proceed now to the final chapter, where we end on an upbeat note by taking a look at what you *can* control. Although you'll never eliminate rejection and criticism entirely, you can do plenty to lessen its occurrence.

Avert Rejection through Superior Business Practices

TAKING CONTROL

Let's take a look at the well-known serenity prayer: "God grant me the serenity to accept the things I cannot change, the courage to change the things I can, and the wisdom to know the difference." The first nine chapters of this book have, I hope, brought home this point: Rejection and customer complaints are inevitable, but you can learn to take them in stride, with serenity.

This book concludes by showing you what you *can* change if you are courageous, creative, and committed to running a business known for superlative customer service and a high ratio of referral sales. You won't escape rejection entirely, but you surely will minimize its occurrence.

WHERE DO YOU WISH TO EXCEL?

Jay Goltz, author of *The Street Smart Entrepreneur,* makes an excellent point:

> I used to think you have to give your customers the best prices, outstanding quality, and exceptional service. Nobody told me: *no* company can give the best prices, outstanding quality, and exceptional service and survive in business very long. Most successful companies usually give two out of three of those things in one combination or another. Discount stores, for instance, provide low prices and good quality merchandise. But the service is nothing to write home about. Federal Express provides excellent service and outstanding quality, but not the lowest prices. *It costs money to provide service and quality.*

TRY THIS!
■ ■ ■

It's tempting to try to do the impossible—provide the best prices, quality, and service. Consider your business goals and where you excel currently. What do you want to be known for—the best prices, outstanding quality, or exceptional service? If you have to choose two out of three, what will it be?   ...!

If you chose best prices and outstanding quality as your two criteria, it doesn't mean that you shouldn't provide excellent customer service. However, you may not be able to offer the *best* customer service in the industry. If producing the highest quality product is important to you, and you want to offer superior customer service, you court failure when you charge the lowest price.

Whichever two achievements you choose, don't let the third one slip away. It's important to keep price, quality, and service in mind at all times to stay competitive. But do choose where you intend to excel.

The remainder of this chapter examines seven key strategies for building a rejection-proof business. If you employ all or most of these strategies, I am confident that you will reduce rejection in the sales and customer service process significantly. If you do even one of these strategies really well, you will make an impact. When you review the strategies, evaluate how your performance measures up. Add to this list additional ideas that you know would make your business more attractive and compelling to your customers. Becoming rejection-proof is an evolutionary process.

1. BE YOUR OWN CRITIC

The best way to better your performance is to be self-motivated to improve, rather than only reacting to customer complaint or competitive pressure. Review your internal practices and your sales and customer service policies and procedures to see whether they bring your desired results. This may seem obvious, but many entrepreneurs are so focused on moving forward and getting their newest products to market, or they are so tied up putting out fires, they spend little time reviewing day-to-day operations and business policies. You can't afford not to spend this time because the clues to better service and sales lie in thinking about the questions listed below.

 **TRY THIS!**

Judge your performance according to the following known strategies for generating successful customer retention and referral sales. Each is followed by something you might hear from a prospect or customer as it relates to that criterion.

1. Can customers reach you or another real person easily when they want to buy your product or register a complaint? If not, have you trained your customers to know what to expect as well as when and how you are most accessible?

   "Your voice mail took me through a maze of options I wasn't interested in. By the time I got to my fifth choice, I couldn't remember the first two. All I wanted to do was speak to someone who would help me with my problem."

2. Are you available during the hours most of your customers need you?

"I installed a new e-mail program on my computer, and it crashed my system. I was furious to discover that your customer service center is open only Monday through Friday, during West Coast business hours. Don't you realize that most of us use e-mail on the weekends?"

3. Do you have a system for contacting your customers regularly to ask whether they are having any problems and to elicit suggestions for improvement?

   "I was impressed when my new-car dealer contacted me six months after I bought the vehicle to see whether I was satisfied. Most car dealerships forget about you a week after you buy the car. I told the salesperson I was happy with everything but the way the horn sounds. He told me he will report my feedback to the company. I like dealing with a car dealership that seems to care about more than just the sale."

4. How rapidly do you respond to customer questions and resolve problems?

   "I was delighted when my computer software manufacturer overnighted me a new CD when the one I tried to install was defective. I explained that my business depends on the software, and the company was immediately responsive. It helped me forgive the nuisance of having to wait the extra day."

5. Do customers like doing business with you and your firm? If so, why? How do you know? Do they tell you and others? How do you ensure an enjoyable experience for your customers? Are most of your customers satisfied, delighted, or enthralled?

   "We ask for customer comments at our restaurants by giving patrons a form to fill out at their tables. We encourage them to take the time to fill out the form by entering each comment card into a random drawing for a free meal. We have been pleasantly surprised by the number of positive comments we receive, and we're able to incorporate many suggestions into our menu."

6. Do you have a system for gathering data on your customers' demographics and buying patterns? Do you have a handle on who your target markets are? Do you operate on assumptions or objective data?

> "Our sales reps sell most air conditioners at night and on weekends because it's usually men who buy air conditioners. They don't want to feel stupid for not knowing a lot about air conditioners, especially if their wives are with them. And they don't want to worry about installing an air conditioner. We make it easy for them. We provide extended evening hours in the summertime and knowledgeable sales staff who answer the questions they don't even know they are supposed to ask."

7. Do you know why prospects aren't buying and customers are leaving? Do you have objective data in a written report that you can study to determine patterns? Do you need new or better systems for reporting this information?

> "We are turned down by most prospects because of our price. Most prospects don't want to pay more than $400 for an office chair. We stopped wasting our time trying to sell to every business owner who needs a computer chair and, instead, focused our marketing on certain kinds of businesses that normally purchase high-quality office furniture. Most of our customers don't repurchase from us because our chairs last years without needing replacement. So we brought that feature into our advertising campaign. 'The only chair you will need to buy for the lifetime of your business.'"

8. What percentage of your total business is referral-based? What strategies do you use to encourage greater referrals from cur-

rent customers? To what extent are your current customers your best public relations campaign?

"We started giving current clients $20 off their next chiropractic visit for every new patient they referred to us. That benefit increased our referrals by about 20 percent."

9. Are you meeting business goals and projections? Are you positioned in the industry where you want to be? Have you created a unique and marketable niche? Do you have a stellar reputation you are proud of?

"We recently were nominated by the local chamber of commerce as one of the best businesses to work for in our region. The nomination gave me and my staff great pride, even though we didn't win the big prize."

10. Does your fear of rejection or unwillingness to tolerate customer complaints get in the way of reaching your goals? If so, what one suggestion from this book can you implement today?

"I knew that cold calling local businesses would increase my sales because all of the businesses around here need office supplies, but I was too shy to approach strangers. I stopped trying to be something I never will be—a salesperson comfortable with cold calling. I joined the chamber of commerce and another professional networking group, and that strategy has worked much better for me because I get to know some of the business owners personally."

As a self-employed professional, you aren't subject to regular performance reviews unless you do them yourself. Asking these questions of yourself and your staff helps ensure that your customer service and sales approaches are optimal.

2. BE PROACTIVE—HEAD OFF COMPLAINTS AND REJECTION BEFORE THEY OCCUR

What I enjoyed hearing most from the 120 business owners and salespersons I interviewed for this book were the creative strategies they use to head off complaints and rejection before they occur. In most cases, these solutions resulted from trouble the self-employed professionals confronted, either common reasons customers didn't buy or the need for creative ways to compete beyond price.

Shift your energy into preventing rejection rather than reacting to it and not only will you be far more successful but you'll enjoy your business more, too. It's more satisfying to prevent forest fires than to run for the hose whenever a hotspot flares up.

Here are two great ideas for stopping complaint and rejection before they occur:

Rick Gardner, president of Private Party Cars, located in Reno, Nevada, rents display space for people who have vehicles for sale. He reduced customer complaints 97 percent with one simple change in approach:

> We guarantee that more people will see a car for sale parked on our parking lot in one day than will see the car as a result of a classified ad run for four days in the newspaper. When I sell a contract, I tell the customer that 80 percent of our vehicles sell within two weeks.
>
> For the first 12 years of our business, my most frequent customer complaint was this: "I haven't had one call on my car!" I would point out that it wasn't our fault; the problem was the customer had priced the car higher than market value. Customers didn't want to hear it. They tried to blame us for the fact that their cars didn't sell. I spent hours arguing with customers over this problem.

We changed our approach after 12 years, and the problem virtually went away. Now we track how many inquiries are made for every car. If four days pass, and no offer or interest has been expressed, we call the customer. We say: "We want you to know that a lot of people have been looking at your car with interest, but they aren't offering to buy because your price is too high." Then we educate the customer about how much we believe he will need to lower his price in order to sell the car.

Because we head off the customer complaint and approach the customer proactively with concern and individual attention, the customer responds with appreciation rather than anger.

Dr. Robert Gottesman, a chiropractor in Sacramento, California, discovered a novel way to lessen the amount of rejection he experiences from first-time clients:

We used to get lots of cancellations. New patients would make appointments with my assistant, but then a large proportion of them wouldn't show up for their first appointments. Most of them are in pain and afraid, and they haven't met me before. Their friends, families, or doctors would tell them nightmare stories about other chiropractors, increase their fear, and talk them out of coming.

Now I call every new client after he or she has made an appointment with my assistant and before the client comes to see me for the first time. People are shocked: "Wow, a doctor called me and wanted to talk to me. He must really care about me." I introduce myself to them, talk with them about their pain and their fears, and tell them what I'm all about. By the end of the conversation, they are feeling so good about me, they never cancel their first appointments anymore.

I've become their friend; people don't reject friends like they do a stranger.

 **TRY THIS!**

Put yourself in your new clients' shoes. Think of how they feel, starting to do business with you and your company. What can you do to help new clients feel more comfortable with and trusting of you, even before the business relationship begins? What are the typical reasons a new client cancels before you even get started? Can you reassure clients that their fears are unmerited before they begin working with you?

3. STAY IN TOUCH WITH YOUR CUSTOMERS

I have heard repeatedly from business owners that one of the keys to success lies in finding a way to stay in regular contact with your current customers. With only so many hours in a day, you may find yourself spending all of your time selling to prospective new customers or responding to complaints and reorders from existing customers. Low on the priority list fall the activities that keep your name and company product in the awareness of your customers, even if they don't need contact with you today. Unknown to you, however, many of those customers may be looking at your competitors, forgetting about your services, not understanding all the other services you could provide—in short, slipping away. Because you spent so much time and money getting the customers in the first place, it only makes sense to budget a portion of your time and money toward keeping the customers on your active list.

Your method of communication will be driven by your budget and the nature of your business. You may send confirming orders and contact customers when you believe they are close to reordering. You might publish a print newsletter or an e-mail newsletter, like I do. You might call a few customers a week, just to touch base, to ask whether you can be of service, or to find out whether they have undergone any significant changes in personnel or business practices since you last spoke. You might send postcards with a special sale announcement.

Mark LeBlanc, a business consultant who hails from La Jolla, California, works with both business owners who want to grow their businesses and salespeople who want to build repeat and referral business. He offers a strategy so simple, yet so on target:

> Identify your supporters and advocates. Understand the difference between the two. A supporter is someone who will respond to a call or request on your behalf—your references, colleagues who admire you, clients who have been satisfied with your work, etcetera. It's great to have a ton of supporters in your life, and all of us have many. Advocates are those people who believe in what you do and have been so positively impacted by what you do, they will refer prospects and clients to you without you even asking. Advocates are your biggest fans in the marketplace, and it is your responsibility to stay connected to them. Helping them understand what you do and who you do it for is critical to the referral process.
>
> Identify your top 25 advocates, then make sure that none of them goes more than 30 days without some kind of communication from you: mail, fax, e-mail, phone call, or in-person visit. It should cost you less than 50 bucks a month, and you'll get most of your referrals from this group.

4. BE A STREETFIGHTER—CREATIVE MARKETING DOESN'T HAVE TO COST A LOT OF MONEY

Besides reviewing your policies and practices to look for ways to head off rejection, you can use literally thousands of unique and inexpensive marketing strategies to give your company a competitive edge. Expand your thinking beyond the traditional brochure, business card, and yellow pages listing. It doesn't have to cost a lot of money, you don't have to be artistically inclined or an expert in writing press releases, and you needn't own the latest in desktop publishing equipment (though none of that hurts!).

Several excellent books offer more creative ideas for marketing your business than you could possibly use in your lifetime. (Look in this book's bibliography for starters.) It takes only a few moments to come up with a great new idea, and you don't have to read these books cover to cover.

Some marketing strategies cost next to nothing yet increase sales dramatically. One of the best examples I ever heard comes from Jeff Slutsky, a dynamic speaker who coined the term "streetfighting" and who entertains his audiences with fabulous ideas for advertising and promoting their businesses without spending a fortune.

One of Jeff's clients was an appliance store up against a frustrating problem. Prospects would take up a great deal of the store sales staff's time learning all about the different features of each appliance, then they would shop elsewhere to look for a better price. Jeff advised the sales staff to stock their freezers with half-gallons of ice cream. As each prospect was leaving the store on a hot July day, the sales staff handed him a free container of ice cream, no strings attached, just for stopping by. Not only did customers leave the store with a good feeling in their hearts, but they were forced to head straight home so that the ice cream wouldn't melt! This clever strategy headed off a great deal of price shopping at the pass. And what did it cost? Just the cost of a half-gallon of ice cream for every prospect—no big deal.

 **TRY THIS!**

It's time to put on your thinking cap—or to grab your latest copy of a hot marketing book for entrepreneurs. Try something new to delight your customers. Launch an atypical marketing strategy that costs less than five dollars per prospect or customer to implement. What can you give away when a customer buys your product or service or shops in your store? How can you make the customer's shopping experience enjoyable?

If you have staff, brainstorm new ideas at a staff meeting—no suggestion is too ludicrous. Remember the half-gallons of ice cream; you never know where a great idea will originate. Consider starting an online newsletter, which costs virtually nothing but your time to produce. Look for ways to increase your value to your target market with a minimal increase in your cost for delivering services. It can be done if you think out of the box. Be a streetfighter, as Jeff Slutsky would say! **....!**

5. INCREASE THE REFERRALS IN YOUR BUSINESS THROUGH GIFTS AND THANK YOUS

The most direct way to reduce rejection in the sales process is to increase the percentage of your business that comes from customer referrals and warm leads. Ideally, you'll expand your business to the point where you respond to customer interest rather than rely on selling to strangers. Doing everything you can to produce a quality product and offer superlative customer service naturally generates referrals from happy customers. However, you can do even more to encourage referrals. Ask for them!

Many business owners are shy about asking current customers for referrals. It's another kind of rejection to fear, even if you know that a customer is thoroughly delighted with your service and might enjoy connecting you with a friend of hers.

Rick Gardner, president of Private Party Cars, had this great idea for encouraging customer referrals:

> Most of our business is referral or repeat business. We utilize a few simple strategies for capitalizing on happy customers' word of mouth.
>
> When we have a buyer and seller here sealing the deal, they are both delighted. The buyer is excited about his new purchase, and the seller is pleased about the money he is receiving. At that moment, we hand both the buyer and seller a set of "Thank you for your business" cards, perforated and wallet size, with "save 10 percent" coupons inscribed on them. We ask them to hand these cards to eight people who might appreciate them. Giving them the cards when they are both satisfied customers works much better than saying, "Please tell your friends about us."
>
> Also, there's a favorite dining spot in town called Famous Murphys. When the sale is complete, we give a $35 gift certificate for dinner to both the buyer and seller, at a cost to us of $20 each. We're spending $40 for two gift certificates that ultimately will be used by four people. Don't you think they are telling everyone they know about how their car dealer gave them a free dinner? What a cheap way to advertise!

When we imagine asking a customer for referrals, we think of the way life insurance salespeople and others in similar professions were trained to ask after closing each presentation: "Can you refer three friends who could benefit from my service?" The salesperson attempted to get the names and phone numbers before he left the appointment. Perhaps this strategy still is used around the world, but it intimidates many sales professionals, who feel pushy and uncomfortable with the approach. A more fun and effective method is to give something to the customer that makes referrals easy and natural.

6. KEEP YOUR WORD AND OPERATE WITH INTEGRITY

Doug Erickson, president of Capitol Modular, Inc., a buildings supplier and commercial contractor in Sacramento, California, summed up his strategy succinctly:

> The number one rule of running a successful business is this: Do everything you say you are going to do! Don't overpromise in order to get the sale. Promise only what you can deliver, and then surprise them with an extra.

Earlier in the book, I relayed Jeff Slutsky's inspirational tale of how he hired a Lear jet to get him to a speaking engagement he committed to—a $7,000 expense coming right out of his pocket. Jeff was determined to honor his word to the client no matter what it cost because integrity was a primary value for him.

David Goldsmith, president of Customer Edge, a consulting firm dedicated to helping business owners improve customer service, tells a similar story:

I was the president of a communications company, CP Communications, that rented wireless microphones and other broadcast equipment. We were renting some equipment for a project in Curacao, and they called to say the equipment didn't work. It was a national holiday there, so we couldn't use overnight mail. We had to put someone on a plane to hand-carry the equipment there. He grew to be one of my top customers, and as the story travelled, we acquired the reputation of being a company that will do whatever it takes.

What if a customer is unhappy with your product or services, but the problem is entirely his fault, not yours? To what extent should you lose money to make a customer happy, even if you or your staff did nothing wrong? Every company makes its own decisions about this matter. Whatever you decide, be consistent and train your staff regarding your expectations. You may decide that an unhappy customer is too risky and you'll do whatever it takes, no matter whose fault it is. The *Daily Service* newsletter reported the following story:

A Phoenix pool builder constructed a $25,000 pool for a first-time customer. When the pool was completed, the customer was unhappy. He had been vague in communicating with the pool builder, but it was important to the builder to make this customer happy. Therefore, he tore out the pool and rebuilt it to the customer's specifications at his own expense.

The customer was shocked—and pleased. He called the Phoenix newspaper and said, "You're not going to believe this." The paper did a front-page story about the builder. The free publicity generated about $200,000 worth of new business for the pool builder. That was the best $25,000 he could have spent!

The pool contractor said it was his ironclad rule of business never to leave the job site until the customer is happy.

Needless to say, he is one of the most profitable pool builders in Phoenix.

TRY THIS!

Do you consider the example above to be too extreme? How far will you go to make a customer happy? Which one of the following statements rings most true for you and your business? None of them is right or wrong; it's a matter of personal preference.

1. When I promise something, I deliver it, or I find someone who can, no matter what financial loss results. I keep my word no matter what.
2. If I overpromise something and realize that I cannot follow through, I apologize to the client and try to help her find an alternative. I don't necessarily honor the commitment if it is too costly or stressful for me to complete.
3. I underpromise what I'll provide for clients so that I never fail to meet their expectations. Then, if possible, I surprise them by giving it to them faster or better than they even asked for.
4. If I make a mistake, I do whatever it takes to remedy the problem. If I did everything right, and the customer is still dissatisfied, I don't feel obliged to lose money or time to make the customer happy. I'd rather spend my energies serving customers who are better suited for my company.

7. EMPOWER YOUR STAFF, AND BE SURE THEY ARE REJECTION-PROOF

The majority of your customers may interact with your staff instead of you. In this case, your staff must be (1) empowered

to respond to customer complaints in a helpful way, (2) courageous enough to enforce company policies, and (3) trained as professionals in sales and service.

Here's an example of what can happen when your staff are not skilled at handling rejection:

I swim laps every day at a local health club. The club has a medium-sized pool that often crowds with too many swimmers at one time. Therefore, certain hours of the day are designated for lap swimming only. During this time, no children are allowed in the pool, making it easier for swimmers like me to get their exercise without maneuvering around screaming, splashing kids.

One summer, I was frustrated by large numbers of families and teenagers who disregarded the rules, intruding upon my lap time and splashing around in the pool when they didn't belong there.

I frequently complained to the office manager of the club, Mary. She was always sympathetic and concerned, promising to straighten out the problem right away. I witnessed her telling staff not to let families into the pool area during designated lap-swimming times. They posted signs around the club reminding families of the designated family swim times. These attempts did not work. Families continued to crowd the pool during nonfamily swim times. One day, I saw clearly what the problem was.

A family of eight turned the pool into their own private party during my lap time. I was maneuvering my way around a bunch of splashing teenagers, grumbling under my breath, when I saw a health club staffer enter the pool area. "Ah, relief is in sight," I thought. "He will throw the families out of the pool, and I can swim my laps without interruption."

That is not what happened. Instead, he joked with the families in a friendly manner, took care of some maintenance tasks, and left the pool area.

I was furious. Then I realized: The rules may be in place, but the staff members don't want to be the bad guys by enforcing them. Even if they receive a slap on the hand from their supervisor for not enforcing the rules, they prefer that level of rejection to the hostility that would result from throwing families and teenagers out of the pool when they were enjoying themselves.

A business's rules are enforceable only if staff members have the proper incentive, training, and self-confidence to withstand the rejection that invariably accompanies telling a customer that he can't have or do something he wants to do. If your business rules aren't being followed, look closely at your staff's behavior. You must give them tools to do their jobs well and positive reinforcement for doing so. Be sure to back up employees on the front line dealing with angry customers. Sometimes an employee enforces an unpopular policy because she does not want negative consequences for her employment. As an inducement to be willing to do something uncomfortable, employees may require discipline for failing to enforce the company's policies. (I would guess, in my pool example above, that staff members suffered no negative consequences for failing to enforce the pool rules; thus, the rules had no power.)

We've all had the frustrating experience of dealing with a poorly trained customer service representative who lacks the ability to solve our problem because he only quotes customer service policy like a parrot or tells us that we must speak with a supervisor. To the extent possible, empower all of your staff to solve customer problems. Companies with reputations for superlative customer service give extraordinary latitude and problem-solving authority to their front-line staff.

Don't expect that you can hire someone for $7 an hour, put her on the phones or face to face with customers, give her a script or a company policy manual, and achieve excellent customer service. Invest time and dollars in training your staff as professionals, and you will reduce the turnover of both your personnel and your customers at the same time.

THE HIGH WIRE ACT OF SELF-EMPLOYMENT

Remember your earliest childhood memories of the circus, when you watched with awe the daredevils balancing on the high wire, hundreds of feet up in the air? They used a safety net to protect them from serious injury if they fell and a hand-held rod for balance and to prevent them from leaning too far in any one direction.

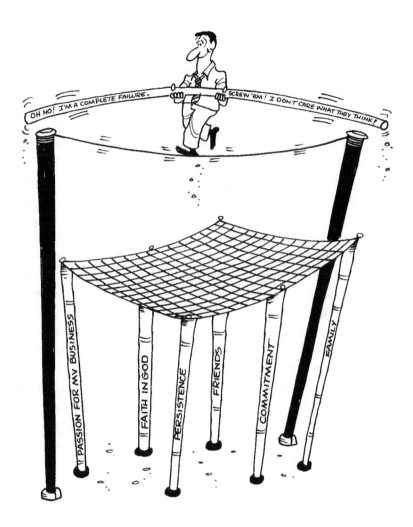

This is a useful metaphor for handling rejection and criticism in your business. Here's the tricky balance you want to achieve:

Lean toward taking rejection and criticism too seriously, and you'll lose your balance. You must respond to rejection with commitment and concern. Learn from it, minimize it when possible, be flexible enough to accommodate circumstances you didn't wish for, listen to customer complaints empathically, but don't lose your perspective. Handling rejection is just another business challenge—nothing more, nothing less. Rejection can break you if you don't surmount your fears, but it is not the monster it is made out to be. It is just another challenge.

Lean toward *not* taking rejection and criticism seriously enough, and you'll also lose your balance. Close yourself off from the lessons rejection can teach you about yourself and your business, refuse to step out of your comfort zone to improve your sales and service skills, or maintain a rigid stance to circumstances that push you in new directions, and you risk losing your business. If you lean too far away from rejection and criticism because of fear or laziness, you miss out on the best vehicle you have for self-improvement.

Throughout your business career, you may lean too far in one direction or another, depending on your self-esteem, mood, and family circumstances; the source of the rejection; and what's at stake at the time. That's okay. That's what the safety net is designed for. Your safety net is your faith in God, your family and friends who love you whether you succeed or fail, your passion and vision for your business, your commitment to do what it takes to succeed and to achieve your goals. If you do fall into that safety net, you can always pick yourself up, climb the ladder back to the high wire, and try it all over again. Rejection may make you lose your step, but it doesn't have to keep you down once you trip. You can always pick yourself up with renewed determination.

In the introduction to this book, I ended the first chapter with the words: "So let's go slay this dragon called "Rejection"— or better yet, let's just come to peace with it instead."

My hope for you is that you come to peace with who you are as well as who you are not and never will be. If you've read this book beginning to end, you know that I believe strongly in accepting our limits. This isn't a motivational book that says you can do anything you want if you just try hard enough. Alas, if that were true, those of us who are always trying would be millionaires by now. We all have limits, even if they are self-inflicted, and it's best to honor them rather than beating ourselves up for not being able to achieve what is impossible for us.

If you never make a cold call or sell your services to a family member, so be it. You still can be wildly successful. If you have trouble hearing customer complaints without taking them personally and feeling hurt, that's okay. You can use that sensitivity to be special in your industry. If the words "rejection" and "criticism" still sound like four-letter words to you, you can learn to accept them, even if they're the part of being a business owner you despise the most. You can take rejection seriously and, paradoxically, at the same time, make it no big deal.

I hope you summon the courage to face your rejection fears. I wish for you the achievement of your dreams and, most important, that you enjoy yourself along the way. Dedicate yourself to improving yourself, but love and accept who you are at the moment—limitations, fears, and all. That's the delicate balancing act that will bring you joy, prosperity, business success, and peace. Befriend rejection, and it will serve you well.

Good luck!

Recommended Resources

BOOKS

Adversity Quotient: Turning Obstacles into Opportunities, by Paul Stoltz, Ph.D. (Wiley and Sons, 1997).

At Your Service: Calamities, Catastrophes, and Other Curiosities of Customer Service, by Hal Becker (Oak Hill Press, 1998).

Being Happy: A Handbook to Greater Confidence and Security, by Andrew Matthews (Putnam Berkley, 1990).

Can I Have 5 Minutes of Your Time? by Hal Becker (Oakhill Press, 1993).

Charisma: Seven Keys to Developing the Magnetism That Leads to Success, by Tony Alessandra, Ph.D. (Warner Books, 1998).

The Communication Coach: Business Communication Tips from the Pros, by Deb Haggerty, Jeffrey Tobe, et al. (Coloring Outside the Lines, 1998).

A Complaint Is a Gift, by Janelle Barlow and Claus Moller (Berrett-Koehler Publishers, 1996).

Conquering the Fear of Rejection: How to Make Yourself Rejection-Proof in Your Sales and Personal Relationships, by Scott Sindelar, Ph.D. (BCFE Clean House Press, 1996).

Customer-Focused Selling, by Nancy J. Stephens, with Bob Adams (Adams Media Corporation, 1998).

The Customer Service Companion, by C. Leslie Charles (Yes! Press, 1996).

Don't Take It Personally! The Art of Dealing with Rejection, by Elayne Savage, Ph.D. (New Harbinger Press, 1997).

Earning What You're Worth? The Psychology of Sales Call Reluctance, by George Dudley and Shannon Goodson (Behavioral Science Research Press, 1995).

Endless Referrals, by Bob Burg (McGraw-Hill, Inc., 1994).

Everyone Remembers the Elephant in the Pink Tutu: How to Promote and Publicize Your Business with Impact and Style, by Mary Maloney Cronin and Suzanne Caplan (Career Press, 1998).

First Things First, by Stephen Covey, A. Roger Merrill, and Rebecca R. Merrill (Simon and Schuster, 1994).

For Writers Only, by Sophy Burnham (Ballantine Books, 1994).

Getting Business to Come to You, 2nd edition, by Paul Edwards, Sarah Edwards, and Laura Clampitt Douglas (Tarcher Putnam, 1998).

Giving and Receiving Criticism: Your Key to Interpersonal Success, by Patti Hathaway (Crisp Publications, Inc., 1990).

The Highly Sensitive Person, by Elaine N. Aron, PhD (Broadway Books, 1996).

Honey, I Want to Start My Own Business: A Planning Guide for Couples, by Azriela Jaffe (HarperBusiness, 1996).

How to Keep People from Pushing Your Buttons, by Albert Ellis and Arthur Lange (Carol Publishing Group, 1995).

How to Stop Worrying and Start Living, by Dale Carnegie (Pocket Books, 1944).

The Joy of Failure, by Wayne Allyn Root (Summit Publishing Group, 1996).

Kaplan Going Indie: Self-Employment, Freelance and Temping Opportunities, by Kathi Elster and Katherine Crowley (Simon & Schuster, 1997).

Let's Go into Business Together: Eight Secrets to Successful Business Partnering, by Azriela Jaffe (Avon Books, 1998).

Non-Manipulative Selling, by Tony Alessandra, Ph.D., Phil Wexler, and Rick Barrera (Simon & Schuster, 1987).

101 Ways to Promote Yourself: Tricks of the Trade for Taking Charge of Your Own Success by Visibility Marketing Expert, by Raleigh Pinskey (Avon Books, 1997).

Prisoners of Belief: Exposing and Changing Beliefs That Control Your Life, by Matthew McKay, Ph.D., and Patrick Fanning (New Harbinger Publications, Inc., 1991).

Rejecting Rejection: How to Take Control of Your Life in Uncontrollable Times, by Bette Price (Kendall/Hunt Publishing Company, 1996).

Reject Me—I Love It! by John Fuhrman (Success Publishers, 1997).

The Sales Coach: Selling Tips from the Pros, by Deb Haggerty, Jeffrey Tobe, et al. (Imago Editions, 1997).

Streetfighting: Low Cost Advertising/Promotions for Your Business, by Jeff Slutsky (Prentice-Hall, 1984).

Success 2000: Moving into the Millennium with Purpose, Power, and Prosperity, by Vicki Spina (Wiley and Sons, 1997).

Take Yourself to the Top, by Laura Berman Fortgang (Warner Books, 1998).

The Tao of Sales: The Easy Way to Sell in Tough Times, by E. Thomas Behr, PhD (Element Books, 1997).

There's a Customer Born Every Minute: P.T. Barnum's Business Secrets, by Joe Vitale (AMACOM, 1998).

Tips and Traps for Entrepreneurs: Real-Life Ideas and Solutions for the Toughest Problems Facing Entrepreneurs, by Courtney Price and Kathleen Allen (McGraw-Hill, 1998).

Tongue Fu! How to Deflect, Disarm, and Defuse Any Verbal Conflict, by Sam Horn (St. Martin's Griffin, 1996).

True Prosperity: Your Guide to a Cash-Based Lifestyle: A No-Fail Blueprint to Get out of Debt, Stay out of Debt, and

Get Ahead, by K.C. Knouse (Double-Dome Publications, 1996).

Turning Feedback into Change, by Joe Folkman, PhD (Novations Group, Inc., 1996).

MAGAZINES

Business Start-Ups, 2392 Morse Ave., Irvine, CA 92714, 800-274-8333.

Entrepreneur: The Small Business Authority, 2392 Morse Ave., Irvine, CA 92614, 800-274-6229.

Home Office Computing: Solutions for Today's Small Business, 411 Lafayette St., 4th Floor, New York, NY 10013, 800-288-7812.

Inc.: The Magazine for Growing Companies, P.O. Box 54129, Boulder, CO 80322, 800-234-0999.

Nation's Business: The Small Business Advisor, 1615 H St., NW, Washington, DC 20062, 800-352-1450.

Success: The Magazine for Today's Entrepreneurial Mind, P.O. Box 3038, Harlan, IA 51537, 800-234-7324.

NEWSLETTERS, AUDIOTAPES, AND OTHER RESOURCES

"The Publicity Hound: Tips, Tricks and Tools for Free (or Really Cheap) Publicity" is a bimonthly subscription newsletter published by Joan Stewart, a media relations consultant, speaker, and trainer with Summit Group, LLC, in Saukville, Wisconsin. The subscription price is $49.95 a year. A sample copy is $3. Contact Joan at 414-284-7451; fax her at 414-284-1737; or e-mail her at jstewart@execpc.com.

Don Peppers and Martha Rogers, Ph.D., authors of the best-selling business books *The One to One Future* and *Enterprise One to One.* If you would like to receive a free copy of the Peppers and Rogers Group's weekly newsletter, "INSIDE1to1," send an e-mail request to subscribe@1to1. com. You also can find valuable resources and materials at the One to One Web site: www.1to1.com. Or contact the firm at 700 Canal St., Stamford, CT 06902, 203-316-5121, or fax 203-316-5126.

Success Networks International, publisher of "Success Strategies," "Success Digest," and "Insight," is dedicated to informing readers and inspiring and empowering them to be their best—both personally and professionally. For a free subscription to "Success Digest," send an e-mail request to majordomo@success-net.com. Use SUBSCRIBE SDIGEST-LIST in the body of the message. Or visit the publisher's Web site for a free trial membership at www. successnet.org. Contact Success Networks International by writing Win-Win Way, P.O. Box 2048, South Burlington, VT 05407, or call 802-862-0812.

"Daily Service," the Internet newsletter published by CustomerEdge, helps people understand how improving relationships with customers can affect their companies' bottom lines. In both a daily and digest format, the newsletter is available through subscribe@customeredge.com.

CustomerEdge, a customer care consulting firm, works with companies all over the world to improve their relationships with customers. For more information, call David Goldsmith, president, at 505-954-4488.

"Don't Take It Personally: Conquering Criticism and Other Survival Skills," by Susan Granger (Dove Audio, 1994).

"How to Vaccinate Yourself against the Rejection Virus!" by Lee Simonson, has become a very popular cassette used in network marketing training programs. Get your new distributors and reps to enter business with their eyes open, and give them the ammunition they need to confront the put-downs, the ridicule, and the rejection they will inevitably face. The audiotape explains how to become immune to the rejection virus. For information, call 800-746-6676.

Hilton Johnson, The Sales Coach, Sales Academy™ (formerly Sales University) "Sales Coaching for People Who Don't Like Selling"™ E-mail: hilton@salesa.com Web site: www.salesa.com virtual sales training and coaching organization. To subscribe to Sales Academy's free monthly "Sales Coach" newsletter and "Hilton's Helper Weekly Sales Tips," send an e-mail message to majordomo @salesacademy.com with the following command: subscribe salescoach-list in the body of your e-mail message. You also may contact Hilton at 224 Commercial Blvd., #303, Lauderdale-by-the-Sea, FL 33308, 954-491-8996, or fax 954-491-7647.

Web cards: If you market any or all of your services via a Web site, Web cards are an inexpensive and creative way to advertise your business. Web Cards, Inc., specializes in Internet marketing, and Web cards are low-cost, full-color, offset-printed postcards with an image of your home page on one side and a custom message on the other. Prices start at $95 for 500 cards. The back of the postcard can be printed with any content you choose. Hundreds of ways to use Web cards exist. For example, a professional speaker can list her top ten speaking topics on the back. A bed and breakfast owner may give postcards featuring a "$50 Off!" sticker to customers who can mail the cards to their friends. A business consultant can use the back of the postcard to promote his products for sale, then mail the postcard to prospects.

Web cards are far less expensive to create and mail than fancy brochures and can be just as, or more, effective.

If you'd like more information about Web cards, as well as some sample cards, e-mail Joe Haedrich at joe@printing.com and tell him that Azriela referred you, or call 800-352-2333.

ADVISERS AND SALES TRAINERS

Dr. Tony Alessandra is the author of several books and audiotape series, including *The Platinum Rule* (Warner Books, 1996), *Charisma* (Warner, February 1998), and *The Sales Professional's Idea-A-Day Guide* (Dartnell, 1996). Contact Dr. Alessandra at 619-459-0197, fax 619-459-0435, DrTonyA@alessandra.com, www.alessandra.com, or www.platinumrule.com. Order products through www.amazon.com or www.alessandra.com.

Hal Becker, author of *Can I Have 5 Minutes of Your Time* and *At Your Service: Calamities, Catastrophes, and Other Curiosities of Customer Service*, offers sales training in power selling, customer service, and sales management. Contact the Becker Group at 6785 Ridgecliff Dr., Solon, OH 44139, 440-542-9884, or fax 440-542-9886.

Linda Blackman, CSP, is an executive coach, a sales trainer, and coauthor of *The Sales Coach*. Linda also is a contributing author to *Chicken Soup for the Surviving Soul* and is featured in the bestseller, *Chocolate for a Woman's Soul*. You can reach her at The Executive Image, Inc., 5020 Castleman St., Pittsburgh, PA 15232, 412-682-2200, www.LindaBlackman.com, or MsBlackman@aol.com.

Bob Burg, author of *Endless Referrals: Network Your Everyday Contacts into Sales* ($14.95, McGraw-Hill) and *Winning without Intimidation: How to Master the Art of*

Positive Persuasion ($14.95, Samark), speaks to corporations and sales organizations worldwide. He also offers audio and video resources based on his books. For more information, call 800-726-3667 or visit his Web site at www.burg.com.

Sandra Crowe is a seminar leader, speaker, and coach who specializes in how to deal with difficult people. She is the author and publisher of the tape series "Snakes, Apes & Bees: A Guide to Dealing with Difficult People" and the book *Since Strangling Isn't an Option*, published by Perigee. She can be reached at Pivotal Point Training and Consulting, 10836 Antigua Terrace, #202, Rockville, MD 20852, 301-984-7818. Her Web site is www.pivpoint.com.

Kathi Elster offers business strategy seminars, partner mediation, and small-business consulting in all areas of business development, with an emphasis on sales and marketing as well as hiring and managing staff. Contact her at 120 E. 34th St., #15L, New York, NY 10016, 212-481-7075.

EntrepreneurPR is a public relations firm specializing in small business. It publishes *Entrepreneur Illustrated.* Contact John Nixon and Scott Smith at 3050 Fite Cir., #209, Sacramento, CA 95827, 916-368-7000, fax 916-368-7008, or iconpub@iconpub.com.

Deb Haggerty connects organizations and individuals through positive strategies in communication, human resources, and technology. Contact her company, Positive Connections, at 2212 S. Chickasaw Trail, #306, Orlando, FL 32825, 888-332-7757, deb@positiveconnect.com, or www.positiveconnect.com

Azriela Jaffe, MBA, BSW. I am a business and relationship coach. I work nationally and coach via telephone and online. One of my specialties is assisting entrepreneurs and salespeople who are procrastinating a key activity because of fear of rejection. Contact me at P.O. Box 209, Bausman, PA 17504, 717-872-1890, or fax 717-872-0963. My Web site for Anchored Dreams® is www.isquare.com/crlink.htm.

Bob Leduc retired from a 30-year career of recruiting sales personnel and developing sales leads. He is now a sales consultant. Bob recently wrote a manual for small-business owners titled *How to Build Your Small Business Fast with Simple Postcards,* as well as several other publications to help small businesses grow and prosper. For more information, contact Bob Leduc at P.O. Box 33628, Las Vegas, NV 89133, 702-658-1707 (after 10 AM Pacific time), or e-mail: BobLeduc@aol.com, subject: "Postcards."

Profnet, Inc., is a Pennsylvania-based corporation that specializes in teaching business professionals how to generate more revenue for their firms. The company does this by setting up Profnet chapters all over the United States and abroad. These chapters allow only one professional from each field as members, so you will find one banker, one lawyer, one printer, one travel agent, for example, in each chapter. Companies are welcome to promote their products and services. The chapters are not sources for finding employment or distributors. The only purpose of the chapters is to learn more information about each business and locate more business for each member. Contact Nancy Roebke at Profnet, Inc., 702 E. 25th St., Erie, PA 16503, 800-214-1999, www.profnet.org, or e-mail: Execdirector@profnet.org.

Sandler Business Institute works with large corporations and individuals. It specializes in sales training and sales management, general management, customer service, and employee profiling. The company provides coaching, training, and reinforcement materials. In Lancaster, Pennsylvania, contact Mark Good, Sandler Business Institute,

600 Old Hickory, #100, Lancaster, PA 17601, 717-560-7972, or Sbi100@aol.com. For other locations, Mark can guide you to the proper office.

Jeff and Marc Slutsky are professional keynote and seminar speakers, authors, and consultants with Street Fighter Marketing, a Columbus-based training organization that specializes in teaching companies how to generate more business on shoestring budgets. They write a syndicated column for the *Columbus Dispatch* called "BizSmart." They can be reached at 800-SLUTSKY (800-758-8759), or www.streetfighter.com.

Robert Sullivan of Information International is a small business and ecommerce consultant. He offers Web site design and hosting services. Contact him at P.O. Box 579, Great Falls, VA 22066, 703-450-7049, or bobs@isquare.com.

Pat Weber is a speaker and trainer who provides keynotes and workshops, presenting ideas and insights to bolster sales and customer relationships. She is the author of *Sales Skills for an Unfair Advantage: 104 Sales Tips to Feed Your Family before You Feed Your Ego.* Phone her at 757-259-1684, or e-mail her at pweber@prostrategies.com.

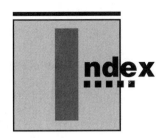

Index

HOW TO CONTACT THE AUTHOR

Azriela Jaffe is the founder of Anchored Dreams®, a national coaching and consulting firm offering practical assistance and emotional support to individuals, couples, and partners in business.

Azriela specializes in relationship counseling for entrepreneurial couples, business partners, and entrepreneurs. She also provides telephone and e-mail coaching for business owners who suffer from rejection phobia or who need a coach to keep them accountable and on track toward meeting their goals. If the strategies offered in this book appealed to you, Azriela can work with you on a short-term basis to help you put them into action.

Azriela welcomes reader response to this book. Contact her at P.O. Box 209, Bausman, PA 17504, 717-872-1890, fax 717-872-0963, or e-mail az@azriela.com or jaffe@lancnews.infi.net.

Visit the Web site for Anchored Dreams® at www.isquare.com/crlink.htm.

Azriela is a seasoned keynoter and workshop presenter and a member of the National Speakers Association. She would be delighted to address your next convention or conference.

She also is the author of the nationally acclaimed *Honey, I Want to Start My Own Business: A Planning Guide for Couples* (HarperBusiness, 1996) and *Let's Go into Business Together: Eight Secrets to Successful Business Partnering* (AvonBooks, 1998).

To subscribe to any of her three free bimonthly online newsletters for entrepreneurial couples and small-business owners, e-mail az@azriela.com or jaffe@lancnews.infi.net. Visit the Anchored Dreams® Web site for information about these newsletters.

To inquire about telephone and online coaching services and professional speaking availability, call 717-872-1890 between 9 AM and 5 PM EST, or e-mail one of the online addresses above.

HOW TO CONTACT THE CARTOONIST

Dave Carpenter started cartooning professionally in 1976, becoming a full-time cartoonist in 1981. His cartoons have appeared in publications that include *Barron's*, *The Wall Street Journal*, *Forbes*, *National Review*, *Good Housekeeping*, *Better Homes and Gardens*, *Woman's World*, *First for Women*, *McCalls*, *Woman's Own*, *New Woman*, *Omni*, *King Features*, *Saturday Evening Post*, *National Enquirer*, *National Business Employment Weekly*, and *American Management Association*. Dave's cartoons also have been published in several *Chicken Soup for the Soul* books.

To contact Dave, call 712-852-3725, or write P.O. Box 520, Emmetsburg, IA 50536.